OLD FAVOURITES, NEW TWISTS

OLD FAVOURITES, NEW TWISTS

100 CLASSIC DISHES WITH A DIFFERENCE

JAMES TANNER

PHOTOGRAPHY BY ANDERS SCHØNNEMANN

KYLE BOOKS

First published in Great Britain in 2013 by
Kyle Books
an imprint of Kyle Cathie Ltd.
67–69 Whitfield Street,
London, W1T 4HF
general.enquiries@kylebooks.com
www.kylebooks.com

10 9 8 7 6 5 4 3 2 1

ISBN: 978-0-85783-091-3

Editors: Emma Bastow and Jenny Wheatley
Designer: Geoff Borin
Photographer: Anders Schønnemann
Home economist: Karen Taylor
Stylist: Liz Belton
Copy editor: Jane Bamforth
Editorial Assistant: Laura Foster
Production: Gemma John and Nic Jones

A Cataloguing In Publication record for this title is
available from the British Library.

Colour reproduction by Scanhouse
Printed and bound in C&C Offset Printing Co. Ltd

FOR ALEXANDRA AND OUR DAUGHTER MEGAN

NOTE ON EGGS

All eggs are medium unless specified otherwise.

ACKNOWLEDGEMENTS

Massive thanks to Kyle Cathie for asking me again
to create another book, and to team Kyle Books
– Emma Bastow, Jenny Wheatley and Catharine
Robertson – for putting it all together. Liz Belton for
the fantastic styling, my main man Mr "Iron Man"
Anders Schønnemann for his epic pictures and
being a legend to work with, and to a very special
lady Karen Taylor who is a top home economist,
Karen I couldn't have done it with out you. I would
also like to thank my big bro Chris who is and has
been my right hand man through thick and thin –
big love to you Bro!, Jax Martin for recipe research,
Sianypie Lane and her super computer! and all the
boys and girls at Tanners Restaurant, the Barbican
Kitchen and Tanners Holdings. Thank you x

CONTENTS

INTRODUCTION

Welcome to *Old Favourites, New Twists* – over 100 of my favourite classic and new recipes from around the world, each with a little twist to make them stand out more than ever. I've covered great British favourites, European classics, Indian flavours and a good old piece of Americana, all shaken up with different flavour combinations to make your taste buds explode!

From small, simple snacks to totally original weeknight meals or elaborate but easy-to-follow dinner party ideas, there's something for every occasion. With an extensive vegetarian section full of tried and trusted big-flavour recipes that are exciting to make and fit for anyone's palate, and some truly show-stopping desserts, these recipes really do have that wow factor and, best of all, they are just a little bit different. Perfect light dishes for a hot summer's day or a warming winter easy slow-cooked roast with a few different ingredients to really shake it up makes for a completely new style of cooking to add to your current kitchen repertoire.

My food inspiration comes from my childhood at home, cooking and experimenting in my mum's kitchen, then moving from there to various professional kitchens around the globe. Here I learnt about classic cookery and new international food. My travels took me not just to new places but new ingredients that inspired me to try exciting new flavours combinations.

We are always learning with food – that's what I find inspiring. I've penned a collection of fantastic, flavoursome recipes that are fit for everyone – whether you're a kitchen novice or an experienced cook, with this book at hand all the hard work is done for you. So, if you want to try an old favourite with a new twist, a classic made totally new or a dazzling dessert to impress, then crank on that stove and get out your kitchen kit because we are going to shake it up!

James Tanner x

SMALL DISHES

WHITE ONION SOUP

Traditionally, brown onions and gruyère are used in a classic French onion soup. I've updated

the recipe by using **WHITE ONIONS** (which gives a sweet, creamy flavour), puréeing them

to give a **SMOOTH TEXTURE,** and serving with **SMOKED CHEDDAR CROÛTONS.**

SERVES 4

70g butter
1kg white onions, sliced
¼ teaspoon ground white pepper
4 sprigs of fresh thyme
1 teaspoon crushed sea salt
200g potatoes, peeled and sliced
100ml dry white wine
1.5 litres good chicken stock
150ml whipping cream
½ baguette, sliced into rounds
150g Applewood smoked Cheddar
   cheese, crumbled

1 Melt the butter in a large saucepan over a low heat and add the onions, pepper, thyme and sea salt. Cook, stirring continually, to prevent the onions from browning, for about 10 minutes.

2 Add the potatoes and wine and simmer gently until the wine has reduced by half. Add the chicken stock and simmer for a further 15 minutes, or until the liquid has reduced and the vegetables are soft.

3 Add the cream and remove from the heat. Purée the soup in a blender and then pass it through a fine sieve to give a really smooth texture. Return to a clean pan to heat through.

4 Preheat the grill to high. Place the slices of baguette on a baking tray and place under the hot grill for about 1 minute on each side or until just starting to colour. Sprinkle some cheese on each toasted round and grill until the cheese has melted.

5 Divide the soup between 4 warmed soup bowls and top with the croûtons to serve.

SPICY VICHYSSOISE

A spin on Vichyssoise (leek and potato soup), my version has a **CURRIED KICK,** making it a real **WINTER WARMER.** To continue the curry theme I thought a dollop of yogurt and a sprinkling of coriander would be appropriate to finish the soup.

SERVES 4

25g butter
2 onions, diced
3 garlic cloves, crushed
2 teaspoons curry powder
3 potatoes, peeled and sliced
4 leeks, sliced
½ teaspoon crushed sea salt
¼ teaspoon white pepper
2 bay leaves
1.5 litres good vegetable stock
natural yogurt and chopped
  fresh coriander, to garnish

1 Melt the butter in a large saucepan over a medium heat, add the onions, garlic and curry powder and cook for about 4 minutes.

2 Add the potatoes, leeks, salt and pepper, bay leaves and vegetable stock and simmer for 15–20 minutes, or until the vegetables are soft.

3 Remove from the heat and take out the bay leaves. Purée the soup in batches in a blender until smooth and then pass through a fine sieve. Return to a clean pan to heat through.

4 Check for seasoning. Divide between 4 warmed soup bowls and top with a spoonful of yogurt and chopped coriander to serve.

CHICKEN CHOWDER

Chowder is an **AMERICAN CLASSIC** and when I worked in New York it was always

cooked with beer, which I've replaced with **CIDER** here in a nod to my West Country

roots. This soup is a great vehicle for leftover meats as well as **SHELLFISH**.

SERVES 4

1 tablespoon olive oil

1 onion, finely diced

1 leek, sliced

2 garlic cloves, finely chopped

300g potatoes, diced

250ml medium cider

350ml good chicken stock

2 boneless smoked free-range
   chicken breasts, cubed

250g fresh clams, well scrubbed

1 tablespoon chopped fresh
   tarragon leaves

198g can sweetcorn kernels,
   drained

100ml double cream

100g smoked cheese (Cheddar or
   Bavarian), grated

1 Heat the oil in a large saucepan over a medium heat and add the onion, leek and garlic and sauté until tender. Add the potato, cider and chicken stock and cook for about 15 minutes or until the liquid has reduced and the potatoes are softened.

2 Now add the smoked chicken, clams, tarragon and sweetcorn. Simmer for about 5 minutes until the clams have opened and chicken is heated through. Discard any clams that remain unopened.

3 Add the cream and cheese and stir until the cheese melts. Season to taste and serve straight away.

NO-COOK TOMATO AND HERB CONSOMMÉ

Classic consommé is made with tomatoes and tarragon. Egg white is beaten in, which

cooks and floats to the top, and then the soup is strained through it. My method cuts

out all that fuss but still delivers an **INTENSELY FLAVOURED, CLEAR BROTH.**

SERVES 4

1kg plum tomatoes
4 sprigs of fresh basil
2 sprigs of fresh rosemary
4 sprigs of fresh thyme
25g caster sugar
4 teaspoons sherry vinegar
rock salt and freshly ground
    black pepper
extra virgin olive oil, to serve

1 Quarter and deseed the tomatoes and place them in a large bowl. Reserve a few basil leaves for garnish. Tear the remaining herb sprigs and add to the tomatoes with the sugar, vinegar and a little rock salt.

2 Crush the tomatoes, with the end of a rolling pin or place in a blender and pulse, until the juices are released.

3 Place a sieve over a large bowl or jug and line it with a muslin cloth. Pour the tomato mix into the lined sieve, enclose and wrap tightly and put a plate or weight on top so the liquid presses through. Place in the fridge overnight to allow the juices to slowly drip through.

4 Season to taste, divide between 4 small bowls, drizzle over a little extra virgin olive oil and garnish with the reserved basil leaves.

RASPBERRY, MANGO AND CHEESE SALAD

A modern take on the pairing of cheese and fruit in a **FRESH** and **COLOURFUL** salad.

SERVES 4

1 ripe mango, peeled and cubed
250g raspberries
110g blue cheese (Stilton or
    Roquefort), cubed
10g basil leaves, torn
6 tablespoons raspberry vinegar
4 tablespoons olive oil
1 teaspoon Dijon mustard
1 teaspoon clear blossom honey
200g mixed baby salad leaves
50g sunflower seeds
crushed sea salt and freshly ground
    black pepper

1 Place the mango, raspberries, blue cheese and basil leaves in a large bowl.

2 Combine the vinegar, oil, mustard and honey in a small jug. Whisk together and season to taste.

3 Pour half the dressing over the fruit and cheese and stir carefully to coat and combine.

4 Place the leaves in a mixing bowl and pour over the remaining dressing, toss until the leaves are coated.

5 Divide the leaves evenly between 4 serving plates and spoon over the fruit mix. Top with the sunflower seeds and serve.

ZESTY POPPYSEED COLESLAW

Prepared with crème fraîche, lime and poppyseeds for a **HEALTHY** and **LIGHT** salad.

SERVES 4

100g crème fraîche
50g mayonnaise
zest and juice of 1 lime
2 teaspoons poppyseeds
1 red onion, finely sliced
½ small white cabbage,
    shredded or grated
2 carrots, grated
8 fresh mint leaves, torn
crushed sea salt and freshly
    ground black pepper

1 Mix together the crème fraîche, mayonnaise, lime zest and juice and half the poppyseeds in a large serving bowl. Then add the onion, cabbage, carrots and mint leaves. Mix and season to taste. Sprinkle over the remaining poppyseeds and serve.

FRUITY GREEK SALAD

I've added **WATERMELON** to the traditional Greek salad to make a **FRUITIER**

VERSION. Watermelon is juicy and sweet – the complete opposite of **FETA** cheese

which is hard and briney. I've also added honey and mustard to the dressing.

SERVES 4

6 tablespoons olive oil
2 tablespoons white wine vinegar
1 teaspoon clear blossom honey
1 teaspoon Dijon mustard
12 mint leaves, chopped
3 baby Gem lettuce
220g cherry tomatoes, halved
1 red onion, sliced
60g kalamata olives, pitted
200g watermelon, diced
100g feta cheese, crumbled
½ bunch of spring onions, sliced
crushed sea salt and freshly ground
   black pepper

1 Put the oil, vinegar, honey, mustard and mint in a small jug. Whisk together, season to taste and set aside.

2 Rip the lettuce leaves and place in a large bowl. Add the tomatoes, onion, olives, watermelon, half the cheese and the spring onion.

3 Whisk the dressing again and pour it over the salad, toss to coat.

4 Divide the salad between 4 serving bowls then scatter over the remaining feta.

WARM TUNA WITH TOMATO KETCHUP DRESSING

Tuna steak is often griddled with tomatoes and olive oil in Mediterranean countries.

I've used tomato ketchup as the base of the dressing for the fish. **TRUST ME, IT**

WORKS! And it makes a great marinade for chicken, too. Brilliant barbecue food.

SERVES 4

3 shallots, finely diced
150ml tomato ketchup
50ml balsamic vinegar
splash of Worcestershire sauce
100ml olive oil, plus extra for frying
¼ bunch fresh chervil, chopped
¼ bunch fresh tarragon,
  leaves chopped
3 new potatoes, cut into ½cm slices
700g sustainably caught tuna loin,
  sliced into 4 steaks
100g rocket
crushed sea salt and freshly ground
  black pepper

1 First make the dressing. Whisk together the shallots and ketchup in a small jug then add the vinegar and Worcestershire sauce, slowly add the oil and whisk until thickened. Stir in the chopped herbs, season to taste and set aside.

2 Heat a splash of oil in a non-stick frying pan over a medium heat and add the potato slices to the pan. Season and turn the slices occasionally, until golden on both sides. Transfer to kitchen paper to drain.

3 Rub olive oil into the tuna steaks and season well. Heat a large non-stick griddle pan over a high heat and sear the steaks for 40 seconds on each side for rare-cooked steaks, if you prefer them a little more well done, reduce the heat slightly and cook for a further 2 minutes on each side to cook the steaks through.

4 To serve, divide the potato slices and rocket between 4 plates, slice each tuna steak in half and place on top of the potato. Stir the dressing well and drizzle over.

QUAIL CAESAR

Everyone knows Caesar salad, and what a great combination of ingredients it is. Why not shake up the recipe by using **ROAST SPLIT QUAILS** instead of chicken, and topping with **QUAIL'S EGGS** rather than the usual hen's eggs?

SERVES 4

6 free-range quail's eggs

2 free-range hen's eggs

2 tablespoons lemon juice

3 garlic cloves, finely chopped

5 anchovy fillets, chopped

5 tablespoons olive oil

2 large slices of bread, crusts removed

4 quail crowns

1 Romaine lettuce

1 tablespoon chopped fresh flat leaf parsley

100g Parmesan cheese shavings

crushed sea salt and freshly ground black pepper

1 Preheat the oven to 180°C/350°F/gas mark 4.

2 Place the quail's eggs in a pan of boiling water and cook for 3 minutes. Remove from the water and place in iced water to cool.

3 Pop the hen's eggs into the boiling water and cook for 3 minutes, then remove and crack into a bowl. The eggs will be coddled (so only just cooked). Smash with a whisk, then whisk in the lemon juice, 2 of the garlic cloves and the anchovies. Slowly whisk in 3 tablespoons of oil, to thicken, season to taste and chill in the fridge.

4 Cut the bread into small squares and place onto a baking tray, drizzle with 1 tablespoon of oil and bake for 15 minutes or until golden brown. Remove and set aside.

5 Season the quail crowns with salt. Heat a non-stick ovenproof pan, add 1 tablespoon of the oil and add the remaining garlic to the pan with the quail crowns, breast side down. Cook gently over a medium heat to add colour to both sides of the breasts. When coloured all over, pop the pan in the oven for about 8 minutes then remove and rest for 5 minutes, lightly covered with kitchen foil.

6 Tear the lettuce leaves into small pieces. Remove the dressing from the fridge and stir in the chopped parsley.

7 Place the leaves and dressing in a mixing bowl and toss to coat the leaves. Divide the salad between 4 serving plates and sprinkle over the croûtons. Shell the quail's eggs, halve and add to the salad. Remove the quail breasts from the crowns (the meat should be moist and slightly pink) and place on the salad. Drizzle any cooking juices over the quail and top with Parmesan shavings.

CHILLI POLENTA MUFFINS WITH CREAM CHEESE FROSTING

I think of these as **TEX-MEX MUFFINS** – savoury cupcakes made with polenta.

Monterey Jack is an American cheese with a **CHILLI KICK.** In contrast the cream

cheese frosting is cool and sweetened with maple syrup. A fantastic brunch dish.

MAKES 12 CUPCAKES

For the cakes

280g fine polenta
80g plain flour
198g can sweetcorn kernels, drained
2 teaspoons bicarbonate of soda
1 large free-range egg
150ml whole milk
100g Monterey Jack cheese, grated
2 green chillies, deseeded and diced
410ml buttermilk
crushed sea salt and freshly ground
  black pepper

For the frosting

30g icing sugar
100g cream cheese
45g unsalted butter, at room
  temperature
1 tablespoon maple syrup
poppyseeds, to garnish

1 Preheat the oven to 200°C/400°F/gas mark 6.

2 Combine the polenta, flour, sweetcorn, a pinch of salt and pepper and bicarbonate of soda together in a large bowl. Mix the egg, milk, cheese, chillies and buttermilk together in a large jug and gently fold into the dry ingredients until just combined.

3 Pour the mixture into a 12-hole cupcake tray lined with paper cases and bake for 20–25 minutes until just firm and golden. To check they are cooked through, insert a cocktail stick into the centre of a cake; if it comes out clean they are ready. Cool on a wire rack.

4 For the frosting, blend all the ingredients together until combined. Spread a little of the frosting over the top of each cake using a palette knife or the back of a spoon and garnish with a sprinkling of poppyseeds.

QUICK PISSALADIÈRE

Pissaladière is a pizza-like dish from southern France which is topped with

caramelised onions. My cheat's version saves you caramelising the onions for hours

on end by using **PUFF PASTRY** and **READY-MADE ONION RELISH.**

SERVES 6 OR
16 AS FINGER FOOD

flour, for dusting
200g all-butter puff pastry
6 tablespoons sweet onion relish
100g plum tomatoes, halved
150g rindless goat's cheese, crumbled
crushed sea salt and freshly ground
    black pepper
fresh basil leaves and extra virgin olive
    oil, to garnish

1 Preheat the oven to 200°C/400°F/gas mark 6. Line a large baking sheet with baking parchment.

2 Lightly dust the work surface with flour and roll out the pastry to about 20 x 30cm. Lay the pastry on the lined baking sheet and prick it all over with a fork. Bake for about 12 minutes until crisp and golden.

3 Remove from the oven and press the pastry down with a clean tea towel. Using the back of a spoon spread the onion relish over the pastry just up to the edges.

4 Season the tomatoes and arrange over the relish. Scatter over the goat's cheese then return the sheet to the oven for a further 5 minutes.

5 To serve carefully slide the pissaladière onto a chopping board. Scatter with the basil leaves and drizzle with extra virgin olive oil. Cut into 6 slices or 16 nibble-sized portions for perfect finger food.

POSH CHILLI AND CHIVE EGGS

Smoked salmon and scrambled eggs is a well-loved brunch dish – with good reason.

Here the two ingredients are combined in the same pan and **GENTLY COOKED**

until just set. The dried chilli adds a touch of **UNEXPECTED HEAT.**

SERVES 4

8 free-range eggs
300ml double cream
25g butter
¼ teaspoon dried chilli flakes
75g smoked salmon, sliced
1 tablespoon chopped fresh chives
crushed sea salt
buttered brown toast, to serve

1 Put the eggs, cream and a pinch of sea salt in a large jug. Whisk well with a fork to combine.

2 Melt the butter in a large non-stick frying pan over a low heat. Add the chilli flakes and allow to infuse in the butter for about 3 minutes, stirring occasionally, or until the flakes are softened.

3 Increase the heat to high, give the egg mixture a good stir and pour it into the pan, cook for 20 seconds or until it begins to set around the edge. Using a wooden spoon, stir and fold the egg mixture from the edge of the pan into the centre.

4 When the eggs are just starting to set, carefully stir in the smoked salmon and the chives.

5 Transfer to 4 warmed plates and serve with buttered brown toast.

RED MULLET ON TOAST

Bored of sardines on toast? Try this instead. Red mullet has quite a strong flavour so

I've combined it with **CRÈME FRAÎCHE, LEMON** and **PEPPERY ROCKET** to

cut against the richness and create a dish that really sings.

SERVES 4

400g new potatoes,
  scrubbed and halved

100g crème fraîche

1 tablespoon chopped fresh chives

1 red onion, halved and finely sliced

4 thick slices rustic bread

2 tablespoons olive oil

4 x 150g red mullet fillets, scaled
  and pin bones removed

squeeze of lemon juice

crushed sea salt and freshly ground
  black pepper

rocket and extra virgin olive oil,
  to garnish

1 Place the potatoes in a pan of salted water, bring to the boil, cover and simmer for about 15 minutes or until tender.

2 Meanwhile combine the crème fraîche, chives and onion in a bowl, season and mix well.

3 While the potatoes are cooking heat a non-stick griddle pan. Brush both sides of the bread with half the oil and season. Fry for around 2 minutes on each side until golden, then set aside.

4 Brush the remaining oil over the mullet fillets and season well. Place the mullet fillets in the griddle pan, skin side down, and cook gently over a medium heat for about 3 minutes then turn over and cook for 1 minute. Squeeze over the lemon juice and remove pan from the heat.

5 Drain the potatoes and stir in the crème fraîche mixture.

6 Place the grilled bread on 4 serving plates and top each with a quarter of the potatoes. Place the hot mullet fillets on the potatoes, scatter over the rocket and drizzle with extra virgin olive oil, to serve.

SAVOURY CRAB SABLÉ

Sablé (shortbread) biscuits are typically stacked up with strawberries and cream to make a pretty dessert. My **SAVOURY VERSION** is presented in the same style but made with **PARMESAN SHORTBREAD,** crabmeat and apple purée.

SERVES 4

For the Parmesan shortbread

100g unsalted butter, cubed
    and chilled
100g cornflour
100g Parmesan cheese, grated
1 free-range egg, beaten

For the lime confit

2 limes
50g caster sugar

For the apple purée

1 Granny Smith apple, peeled, cored
    and diced
1 teaspoon caster sugar
juice of ½ lemon

For the crab mixture

500g white crabmeat
    (preferably from the West Country)
1 shallot, chopped
juice of ½ lemon
1 tablespoon chopped fresh chives
150g good-quality mayonnaise
crushed sea salt and freshly ground
    black pepper
½ handful red amaranth cress
    or baby salad leaves, to serve

1 Preheat the oven to 160°C/325°F/gas mark 3.

2 To make the Parmesan shortbread, place the butter and cornflour in a bowl and rub the butter into the cornflour to form breadcrumbs. Stir in the Parmesan cheese and bind the mixture together with half the beaten egg. Roll out the dough, between two pieces of greaseproof paper, to a thickness of 0.5cm. Chill in the fridge for 30 minutes.

3 Remove the top layer of greaseproof paper and cut the dough into 4 discs with an 8cm pastry cutter. Transfer the discs, still on the paper, to a non-stick baking tray. Bake for 12 minutes. Set aside to cool on a wire rack.

4 For the lime confit, segment the limes by carefully removing the zest and pith using a sharp paring knife. Then cut out the individual segments into a bowl, reserving any juice. Place 50ml water, the sugar and any lime juice from the segments in a small pan and bring to a simmer. Pour the sugar solution over the lime segments and chill in the fridge.

5 To make the apple purée, put all the ingredients with 1 tablespoon of water in a small saucepan, over a medium heat. Cook until softened. Blitz with a hand-held electric blender or in a food processor and pass through a fine sieve. Chill.

6 Check through the crabmeat and discard any shell. Mix with the remaining ingredients and season to taste. Chill well before assembling the sablés.

7 Take 4 chilled serving plates and place a spoonful of the apple purée on each. Use 2 dessertspoons to shape the crab mixture into quenelles and place next to the purée. Lean a Parmesan shortbread against the crab, drain off the lime segments and scatter around. Finally arrange the red amaranth leaves over the crab and serve.

BREADED FISH GOUJONS

JAPANESE PANKO BREADCRUMBS are lighter, fluffier and have a larger

crumb than normal breadcrumbs, and give these goujons a **FANTASTIC CRISPY**

COATING. The oriental edge is carried through with the sweet chilli mayo.

SERVES 4

200g mayonnaise
50g sweet chilli sauce
2 lemon sole, filleted and skinned
70g plain flour
2 free-range eggs, beaten
100ml whole milk
150g panko breadcrumbs
vegetable oil, for frying
crushed sea salt and freshly ground
    black pepper
1 lemon, cut into 4 wedges, to serve

1 Put the mayonnaise and chilli sauce in a small serving dish and stir well. Set aside until ready to serve.

2 Cut the sole fillets in half lengthways, then slice each half into four long strips on the diagonal.

3 Put the flour in a bowl and season. Mix together the eggs and milk in a second bowl and put the panko breadcrumbs in a third bowl.

4 Dip each goujon into the flour, coating it well, then into the egg mix and finally the breadcrumbs. Place on a plate.

5 Heat the vegetable oil to 180°C in a medium, heavy-based pan or deep fat fryer. Cook the goujons, 3 at a time, for 1½–2 minutes, or until golden brown. Remove from the oil with a slotted spoon and drain on a plate lined with kitchen paper. Repeat to cook the remaining goujons.

6 Serve the goujons with the chilli mayonnaise and the lemon wedges for squeezing.

SHELL-BAKED SCALLOPS

Scallops are usually cooked out of their shells, but I've put them back in and

RESEALED THEM WITH PUFF PASTRY. To serve, slide a table knife into

the pastry and pop the shell tops off, breathing in the **AMAZING AROMA.**

SERVES 4

8 whole scallops and 4 whole
  scallop shells
50ml dry vermouth
100ml good fish stock
60g unsalted butter, cubed and chilled
flour, for dusting
180g ready-rolled puff pastry
1 tablespoon olive oil
1 medium carrot, cut into matchsticks
1 leek, white part only, cut
  into matchsticks
5cm piece fresh root ginger, peeled and
  cut into matchsticks
small handful of fresh coriander leaves
1 free-range egg yolk, beaten
1 tablespoon sesame seeds
rock salt or seaweed blanched
  for 1 minute, to serve

1 Preheat the oven to 180°C/350°F/gas mark 4. Wash and clean the scallop shells and set aside to dry.

2 Pour the vermouth and stock into a small saucepan, bring to a simmer and reduce by one-third. Whisk in the chilled butter. Leave to cool.

3 Dust the work surface with the flour, unroll the pastry and cut out 4 strips, roughly 3 x 30cm with 0.5cm thickness. Heat the oil in a frying pan and sauté the carrot, leek and ginger for around 2 minutes until just beginning to wilt, then drain on kitchen paper and cool.

5 Remove the orange roes from the scallops and set aside. Remove any membrane and tough muscle from the edges of the white scallop flesh then slice each scallop horizontally into 3 slices.

6 Divide the vegetables between the 4 shells and scatter over some coriander leaves. Fan a circle of scallop slices (2 scallops per person), in each of the shells and lay two orange roes in the centre of each. Divide the vermouth stock mixture between the 4 shells to moisten and scatter over any remaining coriander leaves. Replace the scallop shell lids, take the puff pastry strips and carefully crimp around the shell edges. Press down the shells to create a seal, brush the pastry with egg yolk and scatter some sesame seeds over.

8 Place 4 small metal baking rings on a baking tray, sit a sealed scallop shell on each ring and bake in the oven for 8 minutes.

9 To serve, arrange a small pile of rock salt or blanched seaweed onto the centre of 4 plates. Place a baked scallop on top.

SHELL-BAKED SCALLOPS (Recipe on page 31)

THAI MACKEREL PÂTÉ

Mackerel pâté with an **ASIAN SPIN.** Fresh mackerel is cooked in coconut milk and enhanced with **CLASSIC THAI FLAVOURS** of lemongrass, ginger and coriander.

SERVES 8 AS A NIBBLE

2 limes

400ml can coconut milk

2 lemongrass stalks, peeled and chopped

½ teaspoon dried chilli flakes

5cm piece fresh root ginger, peeled and diced

½ bunch of fresh coriander, stalks and leaves separated

1kg fresh mackerel fillets, pin bones removed

2 tablespoons vegetable oil

2 shallots, finely diced

1 red chilli, deseeded and diced

2 garlic cloves, crushed and chopped

1 teaspoon turmeric

crushed sea salt and freshly ground black pepper

crispbreads, toast or crusty fresh bread, to serve

1 Zest the limes and put the zest in a large bowl. Halve the limes and squeeze the juice into the bowl with the zest. Reserve the lime shells once juiced.

2 Heat the coconut milk, lemongrass, chilli flakes, half the ginger, coriander stalks and lime shells in a large saucepan. Simmer gently for 3 minutes, then add the mackerel fillets and cook for a further 3 minutes. Remove the pan from the heat and set aside to cool.

3 Add the oil to a small non-stick frying pan over a medium heat, then sauté the shallots, chilli, garlic and remaining ginger until tender. Set aside to cool, then add to the bowl with the lime zest and juice.

4 When the mackerel is cool remove from the coconut liquid using a slotted spoon and add to the bowl with the lime mixture. Strain the liquid through a fine sieve and reserve. Break up the mackerel flesh using a fork and stir in the turmeric and coriander leaves. Place the mackerel mixture in a blender and blend. Add about 300ml of the reserved coconut liquid to help bind it together. Blend to a semi-smooth texture, season to taste. Present in 100ml ramekins or on a large serving dish. Serve straight away or chilled from the fridge with crispbreads, toast or fresh crusty bread.

QUICK CHICKEN LIVER PARFAIT

Chicken liver parfait is **RICH** and **SILKY SMOOTH** in texture. The classic method is to cook it very gently and slowly in a bain marie, but my super-quick version cuts out all that fuss by **USING THE MICROWAVE!** Great for nibbles, with salty crackers.

SERVES 4

200g butter
1 tablespoon port
200g free-range chicken livers, trimmed
1 garlic clove, finely chopped
1 teaspoon chopped fresh sage leaves
1 tablespoon brandy
2 tablespoons double cream
crushed sea salt and freshly ground
  black pepper
salty crackers, to serve

1 Put 25g of the butter and the port into a medium, shallow microwaveable dish, add the livers and garlic. Cover with clingfilm and cook for 2–3 minutes on 700W power, stirring occasionally, until the livers are cooked but still a little pink. Remove.

2 Put the remaining butter in a jug and microwave on 700W power for 1 minute, or until fully melted.

3 Blitz the livers in a blender with 1 teaspoon salt, the sage and half the melted butter, until smooth.

4 With the motor still running add the brandy and cream. Then season to taste. Divide between 4 100ml ramekins, level the surface of the parfait by gently tapping the ramekins and then pour the remaining butter over the top. Chill in the fridge for 1–2 hours until firm and serve with salty crackers.

INDIAN PIZZA BITES

PIZZA GETS THE INDIAN TREATMENT. Spiced chicken, herbs and yogurt

on **NAAN BREAD** – great for a light lunch or quick supper. The mozzarella keeps

the Italian element and brings everything together.

SERVES 4

2 skinless, boneless free-range chicken breasts, cut lengthways into 1.5cm thick strips

150ml natural yogurt

1 teaspoon garam masala

½ teaspoon curry powder

½ teaspoon paprika

2 garlic cloves, finely diced

1 tablespoon vegetable oil

1 onion, chopped

1 tablespoon chopped fresh coriander

4 mini garlic and coriander naan breads

1 x 150g mozzarella ball

crushed sea salt and freshly ground black pepper

1 Mix together the chicken, half the yogurt, the spices and garlic in a bowl, season well and stir to coat. Cover and leave to marinate for 10 minutes, until it reaches room temperature.

2 Heat the oil in a large non-stick frying pan over a medium heat and cook the onion until tender. Add the chicken mix and gently simmer for 15 minutes or until the chicken is cooked and the sauce reduced. Remove from the heat and stir in half the coriander.

3 Preheat the oven to 180°C/350°F/gas mark 4.

4 Lay the naan breads on a non-stick baking tray and spoon on the cooked chicken. Break up the mozzarella with your hands and scatter over the chicken. Bake for 5 minutes.

5 Meanwhile, mix together the remaining yogurt and coriander in a bowl and season.

6 Serve the pizza bites on a warm plate with the yogurt dip.

DUCK BENEDICT

Eggs Benedict is a **CLASSIC BRUNCH DISH** made with hen's eggs and ham.

Here I've used **SMOKED DUCK BREAST** and **POACHED DUCK'S EGGS**

instead, served with a generous dollop of hollandaise, of course. Simply inspired!

SERVES 4

250g unsalted butter
5 tablespoons white wine vinegar
5 black peppercorns
3 large free-range hen's egg yolks
8 free-range duck's eggs
4 English muffins, halved
400g sliced smoked duck breast
crushed sea salt and freshly ground
   black pepper

1 Gently heat the butter in a saucepan until melted. Skim the white foam from the surface with a spoon, remove from the heat and set aside.

2 To make the hollandaise sauce, pour 3 tablespoons of the vinegar into a small saucepan and add the peppercorns. Bring to the boil and simmer for 2 minutes until reduced by half. Remove from the heat, strain and set aside.

3 Place a glass bowl over a large saucepan of gently simmering water. Add the egg yolks and reduced vinegar and whisk vigorously with a balloon or hand-held electric whisk until the mixture forms a foam. To prevent the sauce from overheating, take the pan on and off the heat as you whisk, and scrape the sides with a spatula.

4 Whisk in a small spoonful of warm butter. Repeat until all the butter is incorporated and the texture is as thick as mayonnaise. Whisk in seasoning to taste. Remove the pan from the heat but leave the bowl over the hot water.

5 Bring a large saucepan of water to the boil. Add the remaining vinegar. Bring back to the boil and swirl the water. Poach the duck's eggs by cracking them individually into a cup and dropping them into the pan of swirling, simmering water. Simmer for 3–4 minutes. Remove with a slotted spoon and drain on kitchen paper.

6 Toast the muffins and put the halves on 4 warmed serving plates. Place a spoonful of hollandaise on each muffin half. Arrange the smoked duck on the top, and top with a poached egg. Spoon over the remaining hollandaise and season with black pepper.

SAVOURY CHOUX BUNS

My savoury version of profiteroles, these are perfect for canapés or as a dinner party starter. The choux buns are filled with **CHICKEN LIVER PARFAIT** and drizzled in a **PORT SYRUP** made sweet and aromatic with thyme and rosemary.

MAKES 20

For the pastry

50g unsalted butter, plus
    extra for greasing
150ml water
75g plain flour, sifted
pinch of crushed sea salt
2 large free-range eggs, beaten

For the port syrup

250ml port
50g caster sugar
sprig of fresh thyme
sprig of fresh rosemary
2 garlic cloves, crushed

For the filling

1 quantity Quick Chicken Liver Parfait
    (see page 35)

1 Preheat the oven to 200°C/400°F/gas mark 6. Grease and line a large baking tray with baking parchment.

2 Heat the water and butter in a small saucepan over a medium heat until the butter melts then increase the temperature. As soon as the water reaches a brisk boil, lower the heat again and tip in the flour and salt. Beat quickly with a wooden spoon until the mixture forms a ball and leaves the sides of the pan clean. Remove the pan from the heat and set aside to cool slightly.

3 Add the eggs, one at a time, beating hard until the mixture is shiny and firm. Either spoon or pipe (transfer the mixture to a piping bag fitted with a large plain nozzle) 20 equal balls of the mixture onto the tray. Bake in the oven for 20–25 minutes, or until golden brown and risen. Transfer to a wire rack and cool.

4 Place the port, sugar, thyme, rosemary and garlic in a small pan over a medium heat, bring to the boil and simmer for about 10 minutes or until the consistency is syrupy. Strain the port reduction and set aside to cool.

5 Place the chicken liver parfait in a blender or food processor and blitz until it is smooth. Transfer the mixture to a piping bag fitted with a medium plain nozzle.

6 To fill the choux buns, make a small cross on the underside of each one with a small sharp knife then pipe a small amount of the parfait into each bun. It is best to do this about 20 minutes before serving.

7 Stack up the buns on a serving plate and drizzle with the port syrup.

CHICKEN TIKKA TURNOVERS

I started with the idea of a **GOOD OLD-FASHIONED PASTY** and experimented

with a completely different type of pastry and filling. So here we have tikka-spiced

chicken in a **PUFF PASTRY** sealed sandwich. Simple and delicious.

SERVES 4

1 tablespoon olive oil

1 onion, diced

2 garlic cloves, finely chopped

3 teaspoons tikka curry powder

2 skinless, boneless free-range
   chicken breasts, cubed

400ml can coconut milk

20g fresh coriander, chopped

400g ready-rolled puff pastry

1 free-range egg, beaten

crushed sea salt and freshly ground
   black pepper

1 Heat the oil in a medium saucepan over a medium heat, then add the onion, garlic and curry powder. Cook, stirring occasionally, until the onions are tender.

2 Add the chicken to the pan and stir until browned. Add the coconut milk and simmer gently for 8–10 minutes or until the chicken is cooked and the milk reduced. Add the coriander, season to taste and set aside to cool.

3 Preheat the oven to 200°C/400°F/gas mark 6. Line 2 baking trays with baking parchment. Cut the puff pastry into 4 equal squares roughly 15 x 15cm.

4 Arrange a quarter of the filling on half of each square, leaving a 1cm border around the edge. Brush the edges with beaten egg and bring the two halves together to form a turnover. Press the edges together to seal and crimp with a fork for a decorative finish.

5 Place the turnovers on the prepared trays and brush with egg. Cook for 15–20 minutes until golden brown. Allow to cool slightly before eating. You could also eat these cold, if you wish.

PARMA POTATOES

I've always been fond of **MINI JACKET POTATOES** with a ham and cheese filling.

This recipe turns that idea on its head by putting the **HAM ON THE OUTSIDE** of

the potato to crisp up. Serve as a side with salads or as part of a buffet-style lunch.

SERVES 4

For the potatoes

12 small new potatoes
12 thin slices Parma ham
2 tablespoons olive oil
1 dessertspoon chopped fresh
   rosemary leaves
crushed sea salt and cracked
   black peppercorns

For the dip

100ml sour cream
150ml plain 0% fat Greek yogurt
2 tablespoons chopped fresh chives
½ garlic clove, minced
1 teaspoon lemon juice
pinch of crushed sea salt and twist of
   freshly ground black pepper

1 Preheat the oven to 200°C/400°F/gas mark 6.

2 To parboil the potatoes, put them in a medium saucepan, cover with cold water add a pinch of salt and bring to a simmer. Cook gently for about 10 minutes until just tender, then drain and refresh in cold water. Pat the cool potatoes dry with a clean tea towel.

3 Mould a slice of Parma ham round each potato. Pour the oil onto a baking tray and add the wrapped potatoes. Roll the potatoes over in the oil to coat on all sides and season with pepper.

4 Roast the potatoes for 7 minutes. Turn the potatoes, sprinkle with chopped rosemary and cook for a further 7 minutes or until slightly golden and crispy. Drain on kitchen paper.

5 For the sour cream and chive dip, whisk all the ingredients together, season to taste and serve with the potatoes.

HAM AND CHEESE OMELETTE

A ham and cheese omelette, but not as we know it! Look out for **WHITE STILTON**

if you haven't tried it – the flavour is not as strong as a blue stilton and I've discovered

that it goes beautifully with **SERRANO HAM**.

SERVES 4

10 free-range eggs
100ml whole milk
¼ teaspoon crushed sea salt
¼ teaspoon freshly ground
   black pepper
25g butter
100g sliced Serrano ham,
   torn into bite-size pieces
80g white Stilton, crumbled
1 tablespoon chopped fresh
   curly parsley

1 Preheat the grill to medium.

2 Put the eggs, milk and salt and pepper in a large jug. Whisk well with a fork to combine.

3 Melt the butter in a large 28cm non-stick ovenproof frying pan (large enough to fit all the mixture) over a medium heat. Once the butter has melted add the beaten eggs and tilt the pan to coat the base evenly.

4 Once the omelette is starting to set, sprinkle over the ham and cheese. Pop under the preheated grill for 2 minutes to crisp the ham and soften cheese. Remove from the grill.

5 Sprinkle over the chopped parsley then flip half the omelette over the other half.

6 Slide the omelette onto a plate and cut into 4 portions to serve.

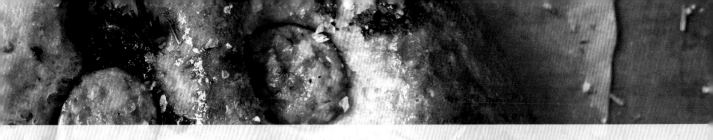

SAUSAGE AND CHEESE LOAF

I came up with this one on **BONFIRE NIGHT** when I cooked it for my daughter

and her friends. I think of it as an **ALL-IN-ONE HOTDOG.** It's massive, so looks

impressive and is ideal for **TEARING AND SHARING.**

SERVES 6–8

1 tablespoon olive oil

300ml whole milk

15g caster sugar

3 x 7g packets of dried yeast

1kg strong white flour, sifted,
　　plus extra for dusting

pinch of crushed sea salt

6 good-quality British sausages

6 tablespoons onion relish

150g Cheddar cheese, grated

leaves from 2 sprigs of fresh rosemary,
　　chopped

1 Pour the oil and milk into a small saucepan with 300ml water and the sugar and heat over a low heat until just warm. Remove from the heat, add the yeast and stir until dissolved.

2 Tip the flour into a large mixing bowl with the salt. Make a well in the centre and gradually add the liquid, using your hands mix to form a soft dough. It may need a little more or less liquid. The dough should be soft, but not sticky. If it is sticky, mix in a little extra flour.

3 Turn out the dough onto a lightly floured surface and knead for 5 minutes. Return the dough to a floured mixing bowl, cover with a clean tea towel and leave in a warm place to prove for 40 minutes (or at room temperature for 1 hour) until doubled in size.

4 Line a baking sheet with baking parchment.

5 Heat a large non-stick frying pan and sear the sausages until they are lightly browned on all sides. Remove the sausages from the pan and cut them into 2.5cm chunks.

6 Knock back the dough and form into a large rectangular shape about 5cm thick. Place the loaf on the lined baking sheet. Using your fingers make deep indentations all over the loaf. Fill some of the holes with the sausage pieces and others with onion relish and scatter over the cheese and rosemary. Cover with a clean tea towel and leave in a warm place for 40 minutes (or at room temperature for 1 hour) until doubled in size.

7 Preheat the oven to 200°C/400°F/gas mark 6.

8 Bake the loaf for 30–35 minutes until well risen and golden. Carefully remove from the sheet and check it is cooked by tapping the base; it should sound hollow. Set aside to cool on a wire rack.

MAINS

SEAFOOD BAKE

A twist on the traditional fish pie format. Instead of the usual mashed potato topping, this one has a **CRUMBLE COVERING** made with **JAPANESE PANKO BREADCRUMBS** to give **TEXTURE** and **CRUNCH.**

SERVES 4

2 free-range eggs

1 small onion, peeled and left whole

1 clove

1 bay leaf

600ml whole milk

500g naturally smoked haddock, skinned and pin boned

1 large leek, sliced into 2cm pieces

50g butter

50g plain flour

50ml Noilly Prat or dry white wine

1 teaspoon Dijon mustard

50ml double cream

1 tablespoon chopped fresh curly parsley

200g cooked, peeled prawns

100g panko breadcrumbs

100g mature Cheddar cheese, grated

crushed sea salt and freshly ground black pepper

1 Place the eggs in a small saucepan of cold water, bring to the boil and simmer for 7 minutes. Remove the eggs from pan and place under cold running water to cool. Peel and cut into quarters. Place in a 20 x 30cm gratin dish.

2 Stud the onion with the clove, place in a medium saucepan with the bay leaf, milk, haddock and leek, bring to a simmer, then set aside for 5 minutes.

3 Remove the fish and leeks from the milk using a slotted spoon. Flake the fish and add it, along with the leeks, to the gratin dish. Strain the cooking liquid and reserve.

4 Next, melt the butter in a small saucepan, add the flour and stir constantly for 2 minutes to make a roux.

5 Stir the Noilly Prat or wine into the roux paste over a low heat, then gradually add the strained milk, stirring constantly. Add the mustard and cream and stir well. Pass through a fine sieve, add the parsley and season to taste.

6 Preheat the grill to high.

7 Place the prawns in the gratin dish, pour over the warm sauce and stir well. Mix together the breadcrumbs and cheese, sprinkle over the top and then pop under the grill for 2 minutes until brown and bubbling.

SEA BASS WITH VANILLA

White fish with white sauce – with a spin. The **FROTHY VANILLA SAUCE** might

sound odd but only half a pod is used so it just **SUBTLY PERFUMES** the delicate

sea bass. New potatoes and spinach are the perfect accompaniment.

SERVES 4

½ vanilla pod
4 tablespoons olive oil
4 shallots, sliced
300ml dry white wine
300ml fish stock
300ml whipping cream
1 tablespoon flour
4 x 180g sea bass fillets,
    scaled and pin boned
juice of ½ lemon
crushed sea salt

1 Cut the halved vanilla pod in half lengthways and scrape out the seeds into a small saucepan. Reserve the pod.

2 Heat 2 tablespoons of the oil in another small pan over a medium heat with the vanilla pod and shallots. Sweat the shallots, without letting them colour, for 2 minutes. Add the white wine, bring to the boil and simmer to reduce to a glaze. Add the fish stock and reduce by half, add the cream and bring to the boil. Pass through a fine sieve and add to the pan with the vanilla seeds. Set aside to infuse.

3 Place a large non-stick frying pan over a medium heat and cover the base with the remaining oil. Season the flour and dust the fillets with the flour. Pat off any excess flour and place in the pan, skin side down. Gently press the fish down with a palette knife for a few seconds (this will ensure they stay nice and flat). Sear for about 3 minutes, then carefully flip the fish over and cook for a further 3 minutes. Squeeze over a little fresh lemon and transfer the fish to kitchen paper.

4 Warm through the vanilla sauce over a low heat and place the fish on 4 serving plates. Froth the sauce with a hand-held electric blender and spoon over the fish to serve.

GRILLED TURBOT FILLET

This is a spin on the **SURF AND TURF** idea. Turbot is a big, strong flavoured fish.

It has a **MEATY TEXTURE** so can stand up well to the **HEARTY ADDITIONS**

of smoked bacon, butter and chicken skin crackling.

SERVES 4

skin from 4 free-range chicken legs
65g unsalted butter
200g button onions, peeled
200g smoked bacon lardons
4 tablespoons olive oil
1 tablespoon caster sugar
200ml red wine
200ml fish stock
400g potatoes, peeled and cut
    into 1.5 cm cubes
2 garlic cloves, crushed
250g wild mushrooms
handful of roughly chopped
    fresh flat leaf parsley
4 x 170 180g turbot fillets, skinned
juice of ½ lemon
crushed sea salt and freshly ground
    black pepper

1 Preheat the oven to 180°C/350°F/gas mark 4. Line a baking tray with a piece of baking parchment. Sprinkle a little salt on the lined tray and lay the chicken skin on top. Melt 15g of the butter and brush it over the chicken skin. Cover with another piece of baking parchment and place a baking sheet on top. Bake for 8–10 minutes, or until golden brown. Remove the skin from the tray and place on kitchen paper to drain off any excess fat. Set aside.

2 Blanch the onions in boiling water for 2–3 minutes and drain, reserving the water. Blanch the bacon for 2 minutes and drain. Place a saucepan over a high heat, add 1 tablespoon of the oil, colour the onions then add the sugar. When the onions are caramelised and golden, add the wine. Bring to the boil and reduce to a syrup. Add the fish stock and simmer until reduced by half. Set aside.

3 Place a large ovenproof non-stick frying pan over a high heat, add 1 tablespoon of the oil and add the potato cubes along with the garlic and cook until the potatoes colour a little. Add the remaining butter and season. Put in the oven for 10–15 minutes or until the potatoes are just cooked, turning regularly. Drain on kitchen paper and set aside.

4 Heat 1 tablespoon of the oil in the frying pan and fry the mushrooms over a high heat for 2 minutes. Add the blanched lardons and cook for a further minute. Season, add the chopped parsley and transfer to kitchen paper. Set aside. Wipe the pan with kitchen paper. Place the cleaned pan over a high heat and add 1 tablespoon of the oil. Season the turbot fillets and lay in the pan. Cook for about 3 minutes on each side. Squeeze over a little lemon juice and transfer the fish to kitchen paper.

5 Put the potatoes, onions, bacon and mushrooms on a baking tray and heat in the oven for 2–3 minutes. Arrange the potato mixture on 4 plates, top with the fish and serve with a little of the sauce. Finish with pieces of chicken skin crackling.

SOLE UNIQUE VÉRONIQUE

Véronique is a creamy white-wine based sauce with grapes and is **VERY RICH.** I've

used tarragon instead of parsley and have added a gratinated polenta crust to give

crunch. Dover sole is traditional but **ANY FLAT WHITE FISH** would work here.

SERVES 4

100g green grapes

20g unsalted butter, plus extra
  for greasing

180g fresh spinach leaves

4 x 600g Dover or lemon sole
  fillets, skinned

1 teaspoon chopped fresh tarragon
  leaves

200ml fish stock

100ml dry vermouth

150ml double cream

100g fine polenta

crushed sea salt

1 Place the grapes in a bowl and cover with boiling water for 30 seconds then drain. Remove the skins – they should fall off easily. Cut the grapes in half, deseed and set aside.

2 Grease a 30 x 20cm deep ovenproof dish or baking tin. Place a large saucepan over a high heat, add the spinach, season with a little salt and add 10g butter, stir the spinach for 30–40 seconds or until wilted. Drain the spinach on kitchen paper, squeeze out the excess water, and put in the greased dish.

3 Season the sole fillets with a little salt. Starting from the thicker end, roll up each fillet neatly and secure by gently pushing in a cocktail stick.

4 Smear the base of a medium frying pan with 10g butter. Put the fish fillets in the pan and sprinkle over the tarragon. Add the fish stock and vermouth. Place on the hob and bring up to a gentle simmer. Cook for about 2–3 minutes and remove from the heat.

5 Lift out the fish using a slotted spoon, drain on kitchen paper and remove the cocktail sticks. Arrange the sole fillets on top of the spinach in the baking dish. Sprinkle the grapes over the fish.

6 Bring the remaining cooking liquid in the frying pan to the boil and reduce by half, add the cream and bring back to the boil.

7 Preheat the grill to high. Pour the sauce over the fish, sprinkle the polenta over and grill for 3–5 minutes, until browned.

SARDINES WITH TOMATO FONDUE, BROAD BEANS AND TOASTED BRIOCHE

This was a starter on our menu a few years ago. People loved it because it was a **POSHER VERSION** of that **COMFORTING DISH,** sardines on toast. The **INTENSELY FLAVOURED** tomato fondue is thick and rich, unlike the tomato sauce you tend to get in your can of sardines!

SERVES 4

8 plum tomatoes
200g broad beans, fresh or frozen
2 tablespoons olive oil
1 shallots, finely diced
2 garlic cloves, finely chopped
1 tablespoon chopped fresh thyme
  leaves
1 tablespoon tomato purée
½ teaspoon crushed sea salt
¼ teaspoon freshly ground
  black pepper
500g passata
2 tablespoons red wine vinegar
12 fresh sardines, cleaned,
  boned and heads removed
juice of ½ lemon
4–8 slices brioche
extra virgin olive oil, to serve

1 Bring a pan of lightly salted boiling water to a simmer, remove the core of the plum tomatoes, cut a cross on the tops and blanch for 30 seconds. Remove with a slotted spoon and refresh in iced water. Add the beans to the boiling water and cook for 3–5 minutes or until tender, drain and set aside.

2 Once the tomatoes are cool, peel, quarter and deseed them. Place the tomato flesh in a bowl and set aside.

3 Heat 1 tablespoon of the oil in a medium pan over a medium heat. Add the shallots, garlic and thyme and cook for 5 minutes. Now add the tomato flesh, tomato purée, salt and pepper and continue to cook for a further 5 minutes stirring constantly. Add the passata, lower the heat and gently simmer for 30 minutes or until the tomatoes have broken up and the sauce has thickened and has an intense flavour. Stir in the vinegar and check for seasoning. Now add the broad beans and stir into the sauce, keep warm over a low heat.

4 Heat the remaining olive oil in a non-stick ridged griddle pan over a high heat. Season the sardines and cook them for about 2 minutes on each side, finish with a squeeze of lemon juice.

5 Toast the brioche and place one or two slices of brioche on each serving plate, top with some tomato fondue and sardines. Drizzle with extra virgin olive oil to serve.

SMOKED HADDOCK REUBEN

Reuben is warm corned beef sandwich and it struck me that the traditional sauce base is

HALFWAY TO A TARTARE SAUCE, which inspired me to pair it with fish instead of beef.

Haddock is a fairly strong fish with good texture so works well with the other **BIG FLAVOURS.**

SERVES 4

4 tablespoons mayonnaise

1½ tablespoons tomato ketchup

½ teaspoon Worcestershire sauce

1 teaspoon grated fresh horseradish
(or creamed from a jar)

1 tablespoon gherkins, drained
and finely chopped

1 tablespoon capers, drained
and chopped

1 fennel bulb, grated

juice of 1 lemon

2 tablespoons vegetable oil

4 x 175g haddock fillets (or 2 fillets
cut in half to give you 4 portions),
skinned and pin boned

25g butter, at room temperature

8 slices rye bread

8 slices of Swiss cheese
(I use American Swiss)

crushed sea salt and freshly ground
black pepper

1 Mix together the mayonnaise, ketchup, Worcestershire sauce, horseradish, gherkins and capers in a bowl, season to taste. Combine the fennel and lemon juice in another bowl, season to taste.

2 Heat the oil in a large non-stick frying pan over a medium heat. Cook the haddock fillets for 2–3 minutes on each side, remove and set aside. Wipe the pan with kitchen paper.

3 Butter half the bread and place the slices, butter side down, on a large sheet of baking parchment on a flat surface. Top each with a slice of cheese and a piece of the seared haddock. Now evenly spoon over the fennel and mayonnaise-based sauce, top each with a slice of cheese.

4 Preheat the oven to 200°C/400°F/gas mark 6.

5 Butter the remaining bread and place on top of the sandwiches, with the butter side up. Return the frying pan over a medium heat. Place the 4 sandwiches in the frying pan and cook for 1–2 minutes until golden brown before turning carefully with a spatula to cook the other side for a further 1–2 minutes. If your pan is not large enough, cook the sandwiches in batches. Place the sandwiches on a non-stick baking sheet and bake for 5 minutes to heat through and melt the cheese. Cut in half to serve.

GRILLED SWORDFISH
WITH NIÇOISE PENNE

I've used swordfish instead of the traditional tuna - a **SIMILARLY MEATY FISH**

with a different flavour. The addition of pasta makes it **MORE SUBSTANTIAL.**

SERVES 4

2 tablespoons extra virgin olive oil

zest of 1 lemon and juice of ½

1 teaspoon Dijon mustard

1 tablespoon chopped fresh parsley

225g dried penne

2 large free-range eggs

100g fine French beans, cut into
   2.5cm pieces

150g asparagus spears

3 tablespoons olive oil

1 red onion, diced

2 garlic cloves, sliced

200g cherry tomatoes, halved

50g pitted black niçoise olives

4 x 180g boneless swordfish steaks

crushed sea salt and freshly ground
   black pepper

1 To prepare the dressing, put the extra virgin olive oil, lemon juice, mustard and parsley in a screw-top jar, season, shake together and set aside.

2 To cook the pasta, bring a large saucepan of salted water to the boil, drop in the penne and cook according to the packet instructions, until just tender. Refresh with cold running water, drain well and set aside.

3 Place the eggs in a small saucepan of water, bring to the boil and simmer for 5 minutes. Place under cold running water to cool. Peel and cut into quarters.

4 Drop the beans and asparagus into a saucepan of boiling salted water and blanch for 5 minutes; they should still retain a firm bite. Refresh in cold water then drain.

5 Heat 2 tablespoons of the oil in a large frying pan over a medium heat, add the onion and garlic, cook for 2 minutes stirring constantly. Next add the beans, asparagus, cherry tomatoes, olives and cooked penne, toss the mixture together until hot. Lower the heat and keep warm on the hob.

6 Heat a ridged griddle pan over a high heat. Sprinkle both sides of the swordfish steaks with the lemon zest, salt, pepper and the remaining oil and sear on the griddle pan for 1 minute on each side. Remove from the pan and set aside to rest for 2 minutes.

7 To assemble, check the pasta mix is heated through, season and add the boiled egg quarters. Arrange the pasta on 4 serving plates, top each with a swordfish steak and drizzle over the dressing.

SEARED STICKY SALMON

Fish is often paired with **WHITE WINE,** either in the sauce or as the accompanying

drink. Here I've used balsamic vinegar instead of wine for the **ACIDIC ELEMENT.**

The dish is finished with sliced garlic, rosemary, baby plum tomatoes and lemon.

SERVES 4

2 tablespoons dark brown sugar
2 tablespoons balsamic vinegar
3½ tablespoons olive oil
3 garlic cloves, 1 finely chopped
   and 2 thinly sliced
zest and juice of 1 lemon
pinch of chopped fresh rosemary
4 x 150g salmon fillets, scaled
   and skin on
24 baby plum tomatoes, on the vine
crushed sea salt and freshly ground
   black pepper

1 Mix together the sugar, balsamic vinegar, 1 tablespoon of the oil, the finely chopped garlic, half the lemon juice and the rosemary in a small jug. Place the salmon in a deep non-metallic dish and pour over the marinade. Cover with clingfilm and place in the fridge for 30 minutes.

2 Preheat the oven to 200°C/400°F/gas mark 6.

3 Place the tomatoes on a baking tray, drizzle with 2 tablespoons of the oil, season and pop in the oven for 5 minutes to soften.

4 Place a large non-stick frying pan over a medium heat. Remove the salmon from the marinade and pat dry with kitchen paper, reserve the marinade. Add the remaining oil to the pan and carefully add the salmon, skin side down. Sear for 2 minutes on each side. Remove from the pan and put the fish on a baking tray and cook in the oven for 5 minutes.

5 Pour the remaining marinade into the pan and heat until reduced by at least half. Add the lemon zest, remaining juice and sliced garlic.

6 Serve the salmon on individual plates with a pile of roasted tomatoes and a little sauce spooned over.

ROAST SALMON ROLLED IN WASABI AND HERBS WITH PICKLED GINGER

Classic roast salmon works really well with a **JAPANESE TWIST.** The **ZINGY**

HERBS stick to the **WASABI COVERING** on the fish, giving it a **REAL KICK.**

Great for a dinner party served with a simple noodle salad and fresh lime wedges.

SERVES 4

For the salmon

2 tablespoons light soy sauce
1 tablespoon pickled ginger, shredded
juice of 1 lime
½ tablespoon toasted sesame seeds
1 teaspoon clear blossom honey
1 tablespoon sesame oil
1 tablespoon olive oil
4 x 140g skinless, boneless salmon
     fillets
50g wasabi paste, or to taste
2 tablespoons chopped fresh dill
2 tablespoons chopped fresh coriander
crushed sea salt and freshly ground
     black pepper

For the noodle salad

1 tablespoon olive oil
½ red onion, sliced
½ red pepper, deseeded and sliced
200g packet fresh egg noodles
2 spring onions, sliced
1 teaspoon sesame oil
1 teaspoon sesame seeds, toasted
1 lime, cut into quarters, to serve

1 To make the dressing, put the soy, shredded ginger, lime juice, sesame seeds, honey and sesame oil in a small jug and stir well.

2 Place a large non-stick frying pan over a medium heat and add the olive oil. Season the salmon fillets and sear on each side for 2 minutes – the salmon should be slightly pink in the centre – then set aside.

3 Lightly spread the wasabi over the salmon fillets. Mix the herbs together and scatter on a plate, then roll the salmon fillets in the herbs to cover all over, arrange on serving plates and drizzle the dressing around.

4 To make the noodle salad, place a wok over a high heat, add the olive oil, onion and pepper. Cook for 1 minute until the vegetables are slightly softened. Add the egg noodles and mix well. Cook for a further 2 minutes, then add the spring onion and sesame oil. Mix together and arrange in a serving dish. Finish with a sprinkle of toasted sesame seeds and serve with lime wedges.

ROAST SALMON ROLLED IN WASABI
AND HERBS WITH PICKLED GINGER (Recipe on page 61)

BEETROOT AND GIN GRAVLAX

Beetroot-cured salmon is becoming trendy as a twist on regular gravlax – it gives the

fish a **STUNNING COLOUR** and flavour. The gin **GENTLY PERFUMES** the fish

but marries extremely well with the earthy beetroot flavours and horseradish cream.

SERVES 4–6

250g raw beetroot
250g coarse sea salt
350g caster sugar
10g fennel seeds
25ml clear blossom honey
2½ tablespoons gin (I use Plymouth)
50g chopped fresh dill, plus extra
    to garnish
1kg salmon side, skin on
100ml whipping cream
25g fresh horseradish, grated
    (or creamed from a jar)
cracked black pepper
rocket and lemon wedges, to serve

1 Wash and peel the beetroot (I prefer to wear plastic gloves for this job!). Dry the beetroot and cut into small pieces. Blitz in a food processor and mix in the salt, sugar, fennel seeds, honey, gin and dill.

2 Pour the gin mixture into a lipped tray and place the salmon on it, flesh side down. Cover with clingfilm, lightly press the fish and place in the fridge to cure for 36–48 hours.

3 Remove the fish, brush off the excess cure and pat dry with kitchen paper.

4 Whip the cream until peaks form, mix in the grated horseradish and season with cracked black pepper.

5 Place the salmon on a chopping board and slice thinly at an angle. Arrange the slices on plates and serve with the horseradish cream, a few rocket leaves, a wedge of lemon and a sprinkling of the chopped dill.

SCALLOPS WITH FIVE-SPICE SAUCE AND SPRING ONIONS

Stir-fried scallops with black bean sauce is a **CLASSIC CHINESE RECIPE.**

I've kept the Chinese element by using a five-spice sauce instead, along with other

STORECUPBOARD INGREDIENTS such as Worcestershire sauce and soy sauce.

SERVES 4

8 spring onions

50ml ketjap manis (Indonesian soy sauce)

1 tablespoon white wine vinegar

1 tablespoon Worcestershire sauce

50ml extra virgin olive oil

30g shallots, chopped

1 teaspoon Chinese five-spice powder

1 teaspoon chopped fresh tarragon leaves

1 teaspoon chopped fresh flat leaf parsley

4 tablespoons extra virgin olive oil

12 large scallops (preferably hand-dived)

½ lemon

crushed sea salt and freshly ground black pepper

rocket, to garnish

1 Bring a small saucepan of water to the boil and blanch the spring onions for 30 seconds. Drop into iced water and allow to cool. Remove and drain on kitchen paper.

2 Put the ketjap manis in a bowl and stir in the vinegar and Worcestershire sauce. Slowly whisk in the oil until it emulsifies. Then add the shallots, five-spice powder and herbs. Season to taste and set aside.

3 Place a ridged griddle pan over a high heat, toss the spring onions in 2 tablespoons of the oil and season. Allow to blacken on the griddle pan, then remove and set aside. Season and oil the scallops with the remaining 2 tablespoons of oil and sear for 30–40 seconds on each side until golden brown on each side. Squeeze a little fresh lemon over the scallops. Drain on kitchen paper.

4 Arrange the scallops on a plate with the spring onions and a spoonful of the five-spice sauce. Garnish with the rocket.

BRILL WITH FENNEL POLLEN

Fennel is a classic partner for fish. So how about using **FENNEL POLLEN** instead?

One of my recent discoveries, this exciting ingredient has an incredibly **INTENSE**

FLAVOUR that really complements brill and most other types of fish. Buy it online.

SERVES 4

2 tablespoons olive oil

4 x 200g brill fillets, skinned (ask your fishmonger to do this)

juice of ½ lemon

10g wild fennel pollen (see introduction)

crushed sea salt

1 Preheat the oven to 200°C/400°F/gas mark 6.

2 Place a large ovenproof non-stick frying pan over a medium heat. Add the oil, season the fish with a little salt and carefully place in the pan, presentation side down. Sear for 3–4 minutes until golden brown. Turn over the fish and transfer the pan to the oven for 3 minutes. Remove from the oven and sprinkle the lemon juice over the fish. Dust the fish with the fennel pollen and serve immediately.

BRILL WITH FENNEL POLLEN (Recipe on page 67)

SAUTÉED SQUID WITH SHERRY PEPPERS AND WARM PRESSED CHICKEN TERRINE

I came up with this idea while eating tapas in Barcelona. A riff on **SPANISH**

SHERRY PEPPERS, teamed with pressed chicken terrine and sautéed squid.

SERVES 4

1.4kg free-range chicken thighs, on the bone

1 tablespoon vegetable oil

2 tablespoons chopped fresh thyme leaves

4 garlic cloves, crushed

1 tablespoon clear blossom honey

1 red pepper, peeled with a vegetable peeler and finely diced

2 shallots, finely diced

1 small red chilli, deseeded and diced

80ml dry sherry

2 tablespoons olive oil

15g butter

500g prepared squid, sliced into rings and tentacles left whole

juice of 1 lime

1 tablespoon shredded fresh flat leaf parsley

crushed sea salt and freshly ground black pepper

extra virgin olive oil, to serve

1 Preheat the oven to 190°C/375°F/gas mark 5. Double line a 450g terrine mould or a loaf tin with clingfilm.

2 Place the chicken thighs in a roasting tin. Drizzle over the vegetable oil, add 1 tablespoon of the thyme and the garlic, toss to coat the chicken thoroughly. Roast for 25–30 minutes.

3 Remove the chicken from the oven and set aside until cool enough to handle. Pick the meat from the chicken, discarding the skin and bones, but reserving the cooking juices.

4 Place the chicken meat in a bowl; add the remaining thyme and honey and the reserved cooking juices. Season and mix everything together.

5 Spoon the chicken mixture, with all the juices, into the lined terrine. Fold the clingfilm over and press down gently. Place a couple of unopened packs of butter (or a suitable weight that fits) on top of the clingfilm to press the terrine down. Chill in the fridge overnight.

6 About 1 hour before serving, place the pepper, shallots, chilli and sherry in a bowl and set aside to marinate for 1 hour.

7 About 15 minutes before serving, demould the terrine, remove all the clingfilm and cut it into 8 slices. Leave to stand at room temperature.

8 Place a frying pan over a high heat and add 1 tablespoon of the oil and the butter. Once the butter is frothing, fry the pepper mixture for 2 minutes, remove from the pan, transfer to a bowl and then set aside.

9 Wipe the frying pan with kitchen paper, add the remaining oil and place over a high heat. Season the squid and sauté for 1 minute, then squeeze over the lime juice, add the parsley and drain on kitchen paper.

10 To serve, divide the terrine slices between 4 serving plates, scatter around the pepper and squid pieces and drizzle with a little extra virgin olive oil.

COD WITH LEMON AND THYME STICKY CHICKEN

Plump fish fillets served with citrus-glazed chicken wings: a riff on the concept of

SURF AND TURF. This has been a **FIRM FAVOURITE** at Tanners since we

first introduced it. The contrast between the textures works extremely well.

SERVES 4

12 chicken wings
200ml good chicken stock
1 sprig of fresh thyme
zest and juice of 1 lemon
1 tablespoon clear blossom honey
3 tablespoons olive oil
4 x 150g cod fillets, skin on
3 garlic cloves, crushed
flaked sea salt and cracked
 black peppercorns

1 Preheat the oven to 200°C/400°F/gas mark 6.

2 Remove the wing tips from the chicken wings. Pour the chicken stock into a large saucepan. Remove the thyme leaves from the stalks and set aside. Add the stalks to the stock along with half the lemon juice and the honey. Bring to the boil. Add the chicken wings and gently poach for 15 minutes. Remove from the heat and set aside for 10 minutes. Then remove the wings from the cooking liquid and drain on kitchen paper. Strain the liquid through a sieve and return to a clean pan, place on the heat and gently simmer until reduced by half.

3 Place a large ovenproof non-stick frying pan over a medium heat and add half of the oil. Season the cod fillets and carefully place in the pan, skin side down. Gently press the fish down to prevent the fillets from curling up, sear for 4–5 minutes over a moderate heat. Transfer the pan to the oven for 3–4 minutes or until the fish is cooked. Reduce the temperature to 150°C/300°F/gas mark 2, squeeze the remaining lemon juice over the fish and return the pan to the oven while you finish cooking the chicken wings.

4 Wipe the frying pan with kitchen paper, place back on the heat, add the remaining oil and quickly colour the chicken wings with the garlic and lemon zest. Add the reduced liquid and stir to thoroughly coat the chicken wings.

5 Remove the chicken wings from the pan using a slotted spoon. Arrange the wings and cod fillets on 4 plates. Return the liquid to the heat and add the thyme leaves, then spoon over the chicken and fish to serve.

ALTERNATIVE SURF 'N' TURF

Another surf and turf idea – this one's **A CORKER!** Pork belly with maple and thyme crackling and butter-grilled lobster both have **REAL BITE,** and the fresh pineapple picks up on the sweetness of the pork belly glaze.

SERVES 4

For the pork

1kg whole pork belly, rib bones removed
1 teaspoon fine salt
zest of 1 lemon
2 onions, roughly chopped
4 garlic cloves, crushed
2 bay leaves
5 sprigs of fresh thyme
4 tablespoons maple syrup

For the lobster

2 tablespoons olive oil
4 split lobster tails
100g butter
juice of 1 lemon
1 small pineapple, finely diced,
    left at room temperature
crushed sea salt and freshly ground
    black pepper

1 Preheat the oven to 220°C/425°F/gas mark 7.

2 Using a sharp knife, score lines around 1cm apart, across the skin of the pork belly, deep enough to just cut through the skin but not through the meat.

3 Rub the fine salt all over the scored skin along with the lemon zest. Place the onions, garlic, bay leaves and half the thyme in a roasting tin. Place the pork on top of the onions, skin side up (this gives the pork great flavour and helps to prevent it from burning on the bottom), and roast for 25 minutes or until the skin starts to look crisp.

4 Reduce the oven temperature to 180°C/350°F/gas mark 4 and cook for a further 2 hours, after which the crackling should be crisp and the meat tender. Remove from the oven and heat the maple syrup and remaining thyme in a small saucepan and then pour it all over the crackling. Leave the meat to rest in a warm place, loosely covered (not too tight or the crackling will go soft) with kitchen foil.

5 Place a non-stick ridged griddle pan over a medium heat, oil the lobster tails and put them in the pan, flesh side down. Cook for 3 minutes. Turn the tails over, add a knob of butter to each one and season. Cook for 2 minutes until the butter melts and bubbles in the shells.

6 Place the tails on 4 plates and squeeze over the lemon juice. Add a wedge of the pork belly and a scattering of diced pineapple to serve.

ALTERNATIVE SURF 'N' TURF (Recipe on page 73)

BARBECUE BAKED BEAN AND CHICKEN CASSOULET

We all know cassoulet as classic **FRENCH FARE,** but it struck me that given the

Tex-Mex treatment, this could be turned into real **COWBOY FOOD.** With the smoky

sweet flavours of the Texan barbecue, you'll want to go back for another ladleful.

SERVES 4

2 tablespoons olive oil

8 boneless free-range chicken thighs, skin on

3 rashers smoked bacon, diced

1 medium onion, diced

1 tablespoon chilli powder

2 garlic cloves, crushed

2 x 415g cans baked beans, drained

200g smoked sausage, sliced into 0.5cm thick slices

3 tablespoons Worcestershire sauce

1 tablespoon dark soy sauce

2 tablespoons white wine vinegar

3 sprigs of fresh thyme

100ml tomato ketchup

50g brown sugar

250ml good chicken stock

1 small red chilli, deseeded and diced

crushed sea salt and freshly ground black pepper

1 Preheat the oven to 200°C/400°F/gas mark 6.

2 Heat a large non-stick frying pan over a medium heat, add 1 tablespoon of the oil and sear the chicken thighs for 1 minute on both sides. Remove from the pan and set aside.

3 Fry the bacon in the chicken oil for 2 minutes until crisp then add the onion, chilli powder and garlic and cook for 1 minute to soften.

4 Put all the remaining ingredients in a 3.5-litre casserole dish. Add the sautéed onion mixture and stir well to combine. Place the sealed chicken thighs on top, put the lid on the casserole and cook in the oven for 30 minutes.

5 Remove the chicken, stir the bean and sausage mixture and replace the chicken on top. Cook, uncovered, for a further 10 minutes. Leave to stand for 5 minutes off the heat before serving.

CARAMEL ORANGE CHICKEN BREASTS

Lemon chicken is a staple **CHINESE TAKEAWAY** dish. Orange adds an

ALTERNATIVE CITRUS TWIST while the salty soy sauce and fish sauce

prevent it from becoming too sweet. This is real **FINGER-LICKING** chicken!

SERVES 4

4 skinless free-range chicken breasts
zest and juice of 1 large orange
2 tablespoons vegetable oil
1 red onion, sliced
4 garlic cloves, sliced
70ml dark soy sauce
100g soft brown sugar
60ml nam pla (Thai fish sauce)
50g toasted cashew nuts, cracked
4 sprigs of fresh coriander

1 Put the chicken breasts in a bowl with the orange zest, add 1 tablespoon of the oil and toss to combine.

2 Place a large deep non-stick frying pan over a medium heat and cook the chicken breasts for 2 minutes on each side, remove and set aside. Add the remaining oil, onion and garlic to the pan, cook for 1 minute, then add the orange juice and the soy sauce.

3 Return the chicken to the pan and coat in the hot liquid, cover, reduce the heat and cook gently for 8 minutes, stirring occasionally.

4 Uncover the pan, add the sugar and turn up the heat. Stir the sauce ingredients together until the liquid has a loose syrup consistency, then add the fish sauce and stir to combine.

5 Arrange the chicken breasts on a warm serving platter with the cashew nuts and coriander leaves sprinkled over.

6 Serve with fragrant rice (see page 80) and Asian greens.

CHICKEN LIVERS WITH POMEGRANATE MOLASSES

Chicken livers are served in the classic French style with a sauce of red wine, verjuice

and brandy. My **AMERICAN-INSPIRED** version uses pomegranate molasses which

is **STICKY AND SWEET** and complements the **IRON TANG** of the chicken livers.

SERVES 4

1 tablespoon olive oil

1 large onion, finely chopped

15g butter

1kg free-range chicken livers, trimmed

2 garlic cloves, sliced

½ teaspoon ground cumin

1 teaspoon crushed sea salt

¼ teaspoon cracked black peppercorns

½ teaspoon smoked paprika

2 tablespoons pomegranate seeds

1 tablespoon pomegranate molasses
   or syrup

juice of 1 orange

1 Cos lettuce

1 tablespoon shredded fresh basil
   leaves, to garnish

1 Place a large non-stick frying pan over a medium heat, add the oil and cook the onion until softened. Add the butter, chicken livers and garlic, cook to seal the livers all over. Then add the cumin, salt, pepper and paprika, mix well and cook for a further 2 minutes. Now add the pomegranate seeds, molasses and orange juice and cook for a further 2 minutes.

2 Snap off individual lettuce leaves, wash and dry. Arrange the leaves on a serving plate and fill with the liver mixture. Serve topped with shredded basil.

SWEET AND SOUR PORK ROAST

Alternative roast pork, **ASIAN STYLE.** To keep with tradition, the pork loin is kept

as a whole piece rather than being shredded, but the **SWEET AND SOUR GLAZE**

and **FRAGRANT VEGETABLE RICE** take it in a **WHOLE NEW DIRECTION.**

SERVES 4

1.5kg rolled boneless pork loin

For the marinade

175g dark brown sugar
60ml teriyaki sauce
60ml dry white wine
60ml chilli sauce
½ teaspoon ground cloves
¼ teaspoon szechuan peppercorns, chopped
pinch of garlic powder

For the fragrant rice

200g jasmine rice
1 star anise
2 tablespoons olive oil
1 red onion, diced
1 garlic clove, crushed and chopped
1 green pepper, chopped
3 plum tomatoes, deseeded and chopped
10g fresh coriander, chopped
crushed sea salt and freshly ground black pepper

1 Combine all the marinade ingredients in a non-metallic dish, large enough to hold the pork, and mix well. Place the pork in the dish and spoon over the marinade to coat. Cover with clingfilm and place in the fridge for 24 hours.

2 When you are ready to cook, preheat the oven to 200°C/400°F/gas mark 6.

3 Remove the pork from the marinade and place in a roasting tin. Reserve any leftover marinade to baste the meat throughout cooking.

4 Cover with kitchen foil and roast for 45 minutes. Baste once with the remaining marinade during cooking and re-cover with the foil. After 45 minutes remove the foil, baste again and cook for a further 10 minutes. Set aside in a warm place, loosely covered with the foil, for 10–15 minutes before carving.

5 Put the rice in a medium saucepan with the star anise, cover with cold water, bring to the boil and simmer gently for 15 minutes or according to the packet instructions.

6 Meanwhile, heat the oil in a saucepan over a medium heat and sauté the onion and garlic until tender. Add the green pepper and cook for about 3 minutes until slightly softened, then add the tomatoes and heat through. Drain the rice and mix with the cooked vegetables. Add the coriander and check the seasoning.

7 Carve the sticky pork loin, drizzle over any cooking juices and serve with the fragrant rice.

FRUITY SPICE-BAKED HAM

Ham and chutney are great partners. The idea behind this dish was to put the chutney inside the whole baked ham. It is **STUFFED WITH DRIED FRUITS AND SPICES**, and roasted with a **MAPLE AND MUSTARD GLAZE.**

SERVES 6

40g butter, at room temperature
2 Cox's apples, peeled, cored and chopped
100g pitted prunes, chopped
60g dried apricots, chopped
1 teaspoon ground cinnamon
¼ teaspoon freshly ground black pepper
3kg smoked gammon joint
20 cloves
2 tablespoons maple syrup
juice of 1 orange
2 teaspoons wholegrain mustard

1 Preheat the oven to 180°C/350°F/gas mark 4.

2 Mix the butter, apples, prunes, apricots, cinnamon and pepper in a bowl and set aside.

3 Take the gammon and remove any string and the rind in one piece. Reserve the rind. Using a long knife make a cut horizontally through the centre of the gammon, then fill with the butter and fruit mixture. Bring the cut ends of the gammon together and secure with skewers. Using a sharp knife score the fat on the gammon diagonally (but not the meat). Place the gammon on a rack in a roasting tin, cover the gammon with the rind and then with kitchen foil and cook in the oven for 1½ hours.

4 Remove the foil and rind. Stud the cloves in the scored rind. Mix the maple syrup, orange juice and mustard and spread over the gammon joint. Add 4 tablespoons of water to a roasting tray and put the gammon in the tray (the water helps to keep it moist and stops the honey from burning on the bottom of the tray). Replace the rind on the gammon and bake for a further 30–40 minutes, basting frequently, until the gammon has a golden glaze and is cooked through. If necessary, add more water during the cooking time.

5 Allow the gammon to rest, covered loosely with kitchen foil, for 30 minutes before carving.

FRUITY SPICE-BAKED HAM (Recipe on page 81)

SUMMER SHEPHERD'S PIE PLATE

I've **DECONSTRUCTED** the British classic so you can taste the individual elements.

My **SUMMERY VERSION** has the addition of broad beans, tomatoes and basil.

SERVES 4

2 tablespoons olive oil

500g good-quality lean minced lamb

½ white onion, diced

1 stick celery, diced

2 garlic cloves, finely chopped

1 teaspoon smoked paprika

1 tablespoon tomato purée

2 tablespoons plain flour

leaves from 4 sprigs of fresh thyme

1 tablespoon Worcestershire sauce

1 tablespoon sweet chilli sauce

1 bay leaf

140ml red wine

200ml good beef stock

500g floury potatoes eg Maris Piper,
    peeled and cut into even-sized pieces

40g butter

4 tablespoons whole milk

100g Chantenay carrots, halved
    horizontally

5 large basil leaves, finely chopped,
    plus extra to garnish

50g Parmesan cheese, grated

60g panko or white breadcrumbs

1 free-range egg yolk, beaten

1 large courgette, diced

100g broad beans, shelled

60g baby plum tomatoes, halved

4 handfuls of fresh spinach leaves

1 knob of unsalted butter

crushed sea salt and freshly ground
    black pepper

1 Place a large saucepan over a high heat, add 1 tablespoon of the olive oil and the lamb. Cook until browned all over, breaking up with a wooden spoon, as it cooks. Remove from the heat and drain in a sieve.

2 Add the remaining oil to the pan and cook the onion, celery and garlic for 2 minutes, before adding the smoked paprika and drained lamb. Stir in the tomato purée and flour, then add the thyme leaves, Worcestershire sauce, sweet chilli sauce, bay leaf, wine and stock. Season, cover with a lid and simmer gently, stirring occasionally for 15 minutes.

3 Meanwhile, put the potatoes in a large saucepan of salted water, bring to the boil and cook for 15–20 minutes or until tender. Drain and mash until smooth. Stir in the butter and milk and set aside.

4 Add the carrots to the mince and continue to cook, covered, for a further 10 minutes.

5 Preheat the grill to high. Mix together the chopped basil, Parmesan cheese and breadcrumbs.

6 Put the mashed potato into a piping bag fitted with a 1cm star nozzle, pipe 4 pyramids of mash onto a non-stick baking tray, brush with the egg yolk and evenly scatter over the breadcrumb mix. Heat the potato under the hot grill for 2–3 minutes until browned, then reduce the grill temperature to low to keep the potato warm.

7 Remove the lid from the mince pan, raise the heat and add the courgette, broad beans and plum tomatoes. Cook, stirring occasionally, for 5 minutes.

8 Place a saucepan over a high heat, add the spinach and a knob of butter, season and sauté for 30 seconds. Drain on kitchen paper.

9 To serve, take 4 warm plates and place a spoonful of the lamb mixture, a pile of spinach and a pyramid of mash on each one. Drizzle any pan juices around and scatter with basil leaves.

TANGY MOZZARELLA LAMB BURGERS

An alternative burger. The **SPICY LAMB PATTIES** taste wonderful against the

more neutral flavour of **MELTED MOZZARELLA.** The standard salad has been

reimagined as a zingy and cooling tomato and cucumber **SALSA FRESCO.**

SERVES 4

For the burgers

2 tablespoons olive oil

1 banana shallot, chopped

2 garlic cloves, finely chopped

juice and zest of 1 lime

1 tablespoon finely grated fresh
    root ginger

¼ teaspoon cayenne pepper

¼ teaspoon Chinese five-spice powder

500g lean minced lamb

1 tablespoon chopped fresh coriander

30g white breadcrumbs

1 free-range egg, beaten

2 x 150g balls mozzarella cheese, sliced

4 floured burger baps, halved

crisp salad leaves, to serve

crushed sea salt and freshly ground
    black pepper

For the salsa fresco

2 spring onions, sliced

½ avocado, diced

2 tablespoons diced, skinned and
    deseeded cucumber

1 plum tomato, deseeded and diced

1 garlic clove, finely chopped

1 teaspoon red chilli, deseeded
    and diced

1 tablespoon sherry vinegar

2 tablespoons extra virgin olive oil

1 Heat 1 tablespoon of the oil in a large frying pan, and sauté the shallot, garlic, lime zest, ginger and spices for 2 minutes. Remove the pan from the heat then add the lime juice, lamb, coriander, breadcrumbs and egg to the pan, season and stir well. Shape the mixture into 4 large burgers, place on a plate, cover and chill in the fridge for 30 minutes.

2 To prepare the salsa, mix all the ingredients together and season to taste.

3 To cook the burgers, heat the remaining oil in a large non-stick frying pan. Add the burgers to the pan and sauté gently for 6–7 minutes on each side, turning occasionally. Transfer to a non-stick baking tray.

4 Preheat the grill to high. Place a slice or two of mozzarella on each burger and cook under the grill until melted.

5 Place each burger on a half bap with some crisp leaves, topped with salsa. Replace the lid of each bap and serve.

BARBECUED LEG OF LAMB

Rosemary would be the obvious partner for a leg of lamb, but this version, with

paprika, honey and chilli has more of **A KICK AND A SWEETNESS.** Cook outside

if weather permits, but don't worry, it cooks just as well in the oven.

SERVES 6

2.5kg butterflied leg of lamb
  (ask your butcher to do this)
zest and juice of 1 lemon
1 red chilli, deseeded and
  finely chopped
4 garlic cloves, chopped
1 tablespoon chopped fresh
  rosemary leaves
1 tablespoon chopped fresh
  thyme leaves
1 fresh bay leaf, shredded (optional)
good pinch of smoked paprika
5 tablespoons olive oil
1 tablespoon clear blossom honey
crushed sea salt and cracked black
  peppercorns

1 Remove any white stringy sinew from the flesh side of the leg of lamb to prevent it curling up and becoming tough. Score the skin with the tip of a sharp knife and place the leg in a large roasting tin. Combine the lemon zest and juice, chilli, garlic, herbs, paprika and oil in a small jug, stir well. Pour the marinade over the lamb and rub in to coat thoroughly. Season with salt and peppercorns and marinate for about 30 minutes.

2 Preheat a barbecue to a high heat. Seal the lamb until coloured and crispy all over, cook for at least 5 minutes on each side. Have a spray bottle of water handy as the flames may flare up as the fat drips. If using a gas barbecue, reduce the heat to its lowest setting or, if using coals, move them to one side of the barbecue and put the lamb on the other side to cook gently, not over direct heat. Cover the lamb with the lid of the barbecue or use a metal bowl, pot or tray. Cook the lamb slowly and gently for 20–30 minutes; it should be slightly pink in the centre. For more well done, simply cook for longer.

3 Remove, brush with the honey and rest, covered lightly with kitchen foil, for a good 10 minutes. Carve and serve, pouring over any juices.

To cook the lamb in the oven: Preheat the oven to 190°C/375°F/gas mark 5. Heat a large ridged griddle pan, roasting tin or large frying pan on the hob and seal the lamb all over – cook for a good 3–4 minutes on each side. When the lamb is coloured and crispy, transfer directly to the oven rack with a tray underneath to catch the juices. Cook for about 35 minutes; it should be slightly pink in the centre. For more well done, simply cook for longer. Remove, brush with the honey and rest, covered lightly with kitchen foil, for a good 10 minutes. Carve and serve, pouring over any juices.

LAMB HOTPOT WITH GREEN SALSA

A British classic from my mother's home county of Lancashire **UPDATED WITH**

SPICES AND SWEET POTATOES and served with a tangy green salsa.

SERVES 6

For the salsa

40g flat leaf parsley

20g mint leaves

zest and juice of 1 lemon

1 garlic clove, crushed

3 anchovy fillets, chopped

120ml extra virgin olive oil

crushed sea salt and freshly
    ground black pepper

For the hotpot

60g butter, cubed

2 tablespoons olive oil

1kg lamb neck fillet,
    cut into 2.5cm pieces

4 lamb's kidneys, trimmed
    and quartered

2 onions, thinly sliced

1 teaspoon ground cumin

1 teaspoon ground ginger

1 tablespoon smoked paprika

1 tablespoon plain flour

4 garlic cloves, finely chopped

3 tablespoons Worcestershire sauce

½ cinnamon stick

1 sprig of fresh thyme

1 sprig of fresh rosemary

1 bay leaf

500ml good lamb stock

1kg sweet potatoes, peeled and sliced

1 For the salsa, put the herbs, lemon zest and juice into the bowl of a food processor, blitz using the pulse action to make a very coarse paste (don't over process). Add the garlic and anchovies and blitz using the pulse action to keep the paste coarse. With the motor running gradually add the extra virgin olive oil.

2 Remove the salsa from the food processor and transfer to a small serving bowl. Check the seasoning. Cover with clingfilm and chill in the fridge until needed. Use within 24 hours.

3 Preheat the oven to 180°C/350°F/gas mark 4. Grease a 3.5-litre lidded casserole dish with 10g of the butter.

4 Heat the olive oil in a large saucepan over a high heat and cook the lamb, in batches, to seal and brown. Remove from the pan, drain in a colander, and set aside.

5 Repeat this process with the kidneys. Add to the colander.

6 In the same pan soften the onions until golden. Add the cumin, ginger, smoked paprika, flour and garlic, sauté for a couple of minutes, stirring constantly.

7 Deglaze the pan with the Worcestershire sauce, add the cinnamon stick, thyme, rosemary and bay leaf. Cover with the stock, bring to a simmer and cook for around 8 minutes until slightly thickened.

8 Cover the base of the greased casserole dish with a layer of sliced sweet potatoes. Season, then add a layer of the browned meat and kidney and then some of the stock. Repeat this process of layers to use up all the meat and stock but reserve enough potato slices to top the hotpot later.

9 Place the lid on the casserole and cook for 1 hour then remove from the oven and carefully take the lid off. Top with a neat overlapping layer of the reserved sweet potato and add the remaining cubes of butter to the layer of potatoes. Cook for a further 40 minutes or until the potatoes are crispy and golden on top.

10 Spoon the hotpot into 6 warm bowls and serve with the salsa.

FIVE-SPICE CALVES' LIVER WITH WATER CHESTNUTS AND CHILLI

CALVES' LIVER is an ingredient you're likely to see offered on restaurant

menus with a rich sauce of mushrooms, brandy and cream, but **ORIENTAL**

INGREDIENTS work really well with its strong flavour. Quick cookery at its best.

SERVES 4

2 teaspoons Chinese five-spice powder

1 red chilli, deeseded and finely diced
   (you can add more, if you wish)

450g calves' liver, cut into strips

2 teaspoons cornflour

50ml dry sherry

2 tablespoons vegetable oil

70g shiitake mushrooms, sliced

225g can water chestnuts, drained

1 tablespoon ketjap manis
   (Indonesian soy sauce)

½ bunch of spring onions, sliced

1 Combine the five-spice powder, chilli and liver in a bowl and mix. Blend the cornflour and sherry together to form a smooth paste, add to the liver mixture and stir well.

2 Place a large non-stick frying pan over a high heat and add the oil. Add the liver mix and quickly cook, stirring constantly, until the liver is seared all over. Add the mushrooms and water chestnuts and continue to cook for 1 minute.

3 Stir in the ketjap manis and sliced spring onions. Cook for a further minute, stirring constantly, then serve on warmed plates.

HIGHLAND BEEF STEW WITH A FILO LID

A modern take on **STEW AND DUMPLINGS.** The carbohydrate element is

provided by the filo pastry lid which is popped on top of the Scotch beef stew just

before serving to keep the crunch. Dare I say it, a **FOOLPROOF RECIPE!**

SERVES 4–5

600g Scottish braising steak, cubed
2 tablespoons plain flour
2 tablespoons olive oil
1 large onion, cut into wedges
2 garlic cloves, finely chopped
300ml red wine
350ml good beef stock
1 bay leaf
2 large carrots, cut into 4cm chunks
2 sticks celery, cut into 4cm chunks
125g potatoes, quartered
100g turnips, quartered
1 tablespoon chopped fresh thyme
   leaves
3 30 x 34cm sheets filo pastry
1 teaspoon chopped fresh parsley
crushed sea salt and freshly ground
   black pepper

1 Preheat the oven to 200°C/400°F/gas mark 6. Line a baking sheet with baking parchment.

2 Season the cubed beef and dust with flour. Heat a 3.5-litre flameproof casserole dish and add 1 tablespoon of the oil. Sauté the onion for 2 minutes then add the beef and garlic and cook until the meat is sealed and browned all over.

3 Add the wine and reduce by half then add the beef stock and bay leaf. Simmer for 30 minutes.

4 Add the vegetables, thyme and a little seasoning then cook in the oven for 1 hour.

5 Brush the filo sheets with the remaining oil, then scrunch them up, roughly to the size of the top of casserole dish and place on the lined baking sheet. Put in the oven for the last 10 minutes of the stew's cooking time.

6 To serve, place the cooked filo lid on top of the stew, in the casserole dish, sprinkle with the chopped parsley, and dig in!

BEEF COBBLER

COBBLERS are more often made with fruit and served for pudding, but here is a **SAVOURY** version with **MINCED BEEF** and **HERBY SCONES** that is quick and easy to make. A great winter warmer.

SERVES 4

For the beef

1 tablespoon olive oil
½ white onion, diced
500g good-quality lean minced beef
1 small leek, white part only, diced
1 stick celery, diced
1 large carrot, diced
1 garlic clove, finely chopped
1 tablespoon tomato purée
2 tablespoons plain flour
leaves from 2 sprigs of fresh thyme
1 tablespoon Worcestershire sauce
1 bay leaf
150ml red wine
200ml good beef stock
crushed sea salt and freshly ground
    black pepper

For the cobbler

300g self-raising flour, plus extra
    for dusting
180g butter, cubed and chilled
1 tablespoon chopped fresh
    curly parsley
leaves from 2 sprigs of fresh thyme
1 free-range egg yolk, beaten

1 Preheat the oven to 180°C/350°F/gas mark 4.

2 Place a large saucepan over a high heat, add the oil and sweat the onion for 1 minute. Add the beef and cook, breaking it up with a wooden spoon, until it is browned all over. Add the remaining vegetables and garlic and cook for a further 2 minutes.

3 Stir in the tomato purée and flour. Add the thyme leaves, Worcestershire sauce, bay leaf, wine and stock. Season, cover with a lid and simmer gently, stirring occasionally, for 15 minutes.

4 To assemble the topping, put the flour and butter in a mixing bowl. Rub together to form crumbs, season and add the herbs and make a well in the centre. Add 3 tablespoons cold water, a little at a time, and mix to form a soft dough. Roll out the dough on a floured work surface, to about 1.5cm in thickness, and cut out 11–12 rounds using a 6cm pastry cutter or the top of a small cup.

5 Pour the beef mixture into a 30 x 20cm ovenproof dish, lay the rounds on top and brush with the beaten egg yolk. Place the dish on a baking tray and bake for 20–25 minutes or until the stew is bubbling and the herby scones are golden.

MIDDLE EASTERN SPICED CÔTE DE BŒUF WITH COUSCOUS

Côte de boeuf is a **DECADENT CUT OF MEAT** – classic French fare. I've given

it a **MIDDLE EASTERN TWIST** by rubbing it with cumin, allspice and cardamom

before roasting, and serving with a **FRUITY HERB AND NUT COUSCOUS.**

SERVES 4–6

For the beef

2.4kg 2-rib piece of beef

3 tablespoons olive oil

2 teaspoons ground cumin

2 teaspoons allspice

2 teaspoons ground cardamom

crushed sea salt and freshly ground
   black pepper

For the couscous

180g couscous

zest and juice of 1 lemon

250ml good chicken stock

10g chopped fresh coriander, stalks
   and leaves

10g chopped fresh mint leaves

60g semi-dried apricots, chopped

20g toasted cracked almonds

100g pomegranate seeds

3 tablespoons extra virgin olive oil

1 Wipe the beef with damp kitchen paper and place in a non-metallic dish. Pour 1 tablespoon of the oil into a small bowl. Add the spices and seasoning and mix together. Rub the spice mixture all over the beef. Cover with clingfilm and marinate for 4 hours in the fridge.

2 Preheat the oven to 200°C/400°F/gas mark 6.

3 Heat the remaining oil in a large non-stick frying pan over a high heat. Add the beef and sear until browned on all sides. Place the beef in a roasting tin and roast in the oven for 1½ hours for medium rare or for 2 hours and 10 minutes for well done, basting after 15 minutes.

4 Remove from the oven and place the beef on a large warm serving dish. Cover with kitchen foil and leave to rest for 15 minutes.

5 While it rests, put the couscous and lemon zest in a large bowl and season. Heat the chicken stock until boiling, then pour over the couscous. Cover with clingfilm and leave for 10–15 minutes undisturbed, then use a fork to fluff up the couscous; don't stir it with a spoon as the grains will stick together. Now add the remaining ingredients and season to taste.

6 Carve the beef, drizzle over any juices and serve with the couscous.

VEAL BOLOGNESE

Using veal instead of the traditional beef gives a **LOVELY STRONG FLAVOUR** to

the Bolognese. You can also add chopped fresh basil leaves or freshly ground nutmeg

to give the sauce a wonderful **FRESH TASTE.**

SERVES 4

25g butter
2 tablespoons olive oil
1 medium onion, diced
2 carrots, finely chopped
2 sticks celery, finely diced
3 garlic cloves, finely chopped
500g veal loin, minced
3 tablespoons tomato purée
250ml red wine
½ teaspoon dried chilli flakes or to taste
400g can chopped plum tomatoes
450g dried spaghetti
100g Parmesan cheese, grated
crushed sea salt and freshly ground
   black pepper

1 Heat the butter and oil in a large saucepan, over a medium heat. When the butter is frothing add the onion, carrots, celery and garlic. Sauté for 10 minutes, stirring constantly.

2 Add the veal and cook, stirring occasionally, for about 5 minutes, until the meat is no longer pink.

3 Add the tomato purée and cook for a further minute. Next add the wine and cook until almost completely evaporated, stirring regularly.

4 Add the chilli flakes and tomatoes, season and lower the heat. Simmer gently, stirring occasionally, for 15 minutes.

5 Meanwhile, cook the spaghetti. Bring a large saucepan of salted water to the boil, add the pasta and cook according to the packet instructions (about 10 minutes). Drain the pasta and divide between 4 plates or bowls, top with the sauce and serve with the grated Parmesan.

MUSTARD AND MAPLE-GLAZED VEAL CHOPS

Veal chops are all too often cooked with honey and wholegrain mustard. Here they

get the **SOUTHERN AMERICAN TREATMENT** with a zingy mustard and sweet

maple syrup glaze. Coleslaw and fresh corn on the cob go particularly well with this.

SERVES 4

4 boneless thick-cut veal chops
100ml maple syrup
4 tablespoons Worcestershire sauce
4 tablespoons wholegrain mustard
3 tablespoons vegetable oil
4 tablespoons soy sauce
1 teaspoon paprika
3 tablespoons soft dark brown sugar
crushed sea salt and cracked
  black peppercorns

1 Season the veal chops on both sides and place in a deep non-metallic dish in a single layer. Mix the remaining ingredients in a jug and stir well to combine. Pour the marinade over the chops, cover with clingfilm and place in the fridge for 6 hours.

2 Preheat the oven to 200°C/400°F/gas mark 6. Remove the chops from the fridge and leave at room temperature for 1 hour.

3 Preheat a ridged griddle pan and sear the chops for 3–4 minutes on each side until they are caramelised. Brush over the marinade then place in a non-stick roastng tin and finish cooking in the oven for 15 minutes (if you prefer your meat well done, cook for a further 10 minutes).

4 Remove from the oven and place on a wire rack to rest for 5–10 minutes, covered with kitchen foil. Slice and serve.

RABBIT AND CIDER COTTAGE PIE

Here rabbit is used in a **DIFFERENT FORMAT** to what we are used to seeing.

Tender cooked boneless pieces of rabbit with vegetables in a **RICH CIDER GRAVY,**

served up as a **COMFORTING** cottage pie – what's not to love?

SERVES 4

1kg floury potatoes (eg Maris Piper),
    cut into even-sized pieces

100g unsalted butter

150g smoked bacon, cut into
    bite-sized pieces

1 large rabbit (about 2kg), meat
    removed and cut into bite-sized
    pieces (ask your butcher to do this)

1 large onion, diced

200g carrots, chopped

200g leeks, chopped

2 garlic cloves, chopped

250ml medium cider

500ml good beef stock

1 teaspoon cornflour

1 sprig of fresh thyme

crushed sea salt and cracked
    black peppercorns

1 Put the potatoes in a large saucepan of salted water, bring to the boil, cover and simmer for 15–20 minutes or until tender. Drain the potatoes thoroughly and pass through a potato ricer or mash with a potato masher. Add 80g of the butter, beat well, season to taste and set aside.

2 Place a large saucepan over a high heat. Fry the bacon pieces for 3 minutes, then add the rabbit pieces and fry for a further 3 minutes or until slightly browned. Remove the rabbit and bacon with a slotted spoon and drain in a colander.

3 Return the pan over a medium heat and melt half the remaining butter. Add the onion, carrots, leeks and garlic and sauté for 2 minutes. Remove the vegetables with a slotted spoon and put in the colander with the meat. Place the pan back on the hob over a high heat, deglaze the pan with the cider and add the stock. Bring to the boil and add the rabbit, bacon and vegetables.

4 Mix the cornflour with a little water to form a paste and add to the pan, stirring well to thicken the gravy. Add the thyme sprig and gently simmer for 5 minutes. Remove the thyme sprig.

5 Preheat the oven to 180°C/350°F/gas mark 4.

6 Transfer the rabbit mixture to a 25cm oval pie dish. Spoon or pipe the potatoes on top. Melt the remaining butter and drizzle it over the potatoes. Cook in the oven for 45 minutes or until the potatoes are golden brown.

VENISON WITH COCOA NIBS AND ALMONDS

Venison and chocolate are a **CLASSIC FLAVOUR COMBINATION.** In this

recipe the chocolate is in form of cocoa nibs, which, along with the almonds create a

CRUNCHY COATING for the meat. Perfect served with red cabbage and parsnips.

SERVES 4

100g nibbed almonds
100g cocoa nibs
4 x 200g venison fillets, trimmed
2 tablespoons groundnut oil
10g unsalted butter
20g clear blossom honey
crushed sea salt and freshly ground
    black pepper

1 Preheat the oven to 200°C/400°F/gas mark 6.

2 Spread the almonds on a baking tray and roast in the oven for 3–4 minutes. Place in a bowl, add the cocoa nibs, and set aside.

3 Rub the venison with 1 tablespoon oil and season all over. Heat the remaining oil and the butter in a large ovenproof frying pan and carefully sear the venison fillets on each side.

4 Transfer the pan to the oven for 5–7 minutes for medium-rare, or for well done cook for 15 minutes, turning twice during the cooking process. Remove the venison from the pan and allow to rest on a wire rack.

5 Place the pan back on the hob over a low heat and add a splash of water and the honey. Once the honey has melted, remove from the heat and add the venison fillets. Ensure that the meat is well coated. Remove and roll each fillet in the cocoa nib and almond mixture.

6 Slice each fillet into 4–6 pieces and serve on warmed plates.

VEGETARIAN

TWISTS

MAPLE-GLAZED GOAT'S CHEESE AND PESTO ON TOAST

This **SPANISH-INSPIRED** snack is so much more than just cheese on toast,

but equally **SIMPLE TO MAKE**. The maple syrup works well with the salty goat's

cheese and pungent pesto.

SERVES 4

200g rindless goat's cheese log
6 sun-blush tomatoes, chopped
4 slices of brioche
4 tablespoons green pesto
2 tablespoons maple syrup
1 handful of rocket
1 tablespoon extra virgin olive oil
1 tablespoon balsamic vinegar
cracked black pepper

1 Crumble the goat's cheese in a bowl, add the sun-blush tomatoes and a twist of cracked black pepper.

2 Preheat the grill to medium and toast the brioche on both sides until golden. Remove and cool. Spread a thin layer of pesto on one side of each piece of toast, spreading it right to the edges.

3 Place the cheese mixture over the toast, drizzle with maple syrup and grill until just slightly melted. Transfer to serving plates.

4 Dress the rocket with the oil and vinegar, and scatter over the toast. Drizzle over any remaining dressing and serve.

ZESTY, SMASHED AVOCADO WRAPS

Guacamole reworked. Here the fresh, bright Mexican flavours with a kick – **LIME, CHILLI AND AVOCADO** – are rolled up in crispy lettuce and warmed tortillas. These wraps make a great party dish.

SERVES 4

2 large, ripe Hass avocados, stoned, peeled and mashed

zest and juice of 1 lime

1 green chilli, deseeded and finely chopped

1 garlic clove, finely chopped

2 spring onions, sliced

1 tablespoon chopped fresh coriander

Tabasco sauce, to taste

4 Little Gem lettuce leaves

1 plum tomato, deseeded and diced

1 tablespoon olive oil

4 wheat tortillas

crushed sea salt and freshly ground black pepper

sour cream, to serve

1 Mix together the avocado, lime zest and juice, chilli, garlic, spring onions, coriander and a dash of Tabasco, to taste.

2 Divide the mixture between the Little Gem leaves and sprinkle over the diced tomato. Season to taste.

3 Heat a large, non-stick frying pan over a medium heat, add the oil and fry the tortillas for around 30 seconds on each side until slightly coloured.

4 Place a filled lettuce leaf on each warmed tortilla and roll up. Serve whole or cut into quarters and eat as finger food, with sour cream for dipping.

THE VEGETARIAN MEXICAN

A filling, spicy dish with classic Mexican ingredients, topped off with **CHEESY TORTILLA CHIPS.** I've also included some vegetables you wouldn't normally find in Mexican food – **FENNEL** and **ARTICHOKE HEARTS** – to produce something a little bit different.

SERVES 4

1 tablespoon vegetable oil

1 large yellow pepper, deseeded and cut into chunks

1 large courgette, thickly sliced

1 red onion, cut into wedges

3 garlic cloves, finely chopped

½ head of fennel, thinly sliced

1 teaspoon mild or hot chilli powder

½ teaspoon ground cumin

½ teaspoon smoked paprika

1 tablespoon chopped fresh oregano or ½ teaspoon dried oregano

1 x 400g can kidney beans, drained and rinsed

1 x 380g can artichoke hearts, drained and halved

1 x 400g can chopped plum tomatoes

1 tablespoon pre-sliced green jalapeños (from a jar), drained (optional)

70g pitted black olives, sliced

100g tortilla chips

180g Monterey Jack cheese, grated

sour cream and sliced iceberg lettuce, to serve

1 Place a large saucepan over a medium heat, add the oil and then the pepper, courgette, onion, garlic and fennel. Mix the vegetables in the hot oil then stir in the chilli powder, cumin, paprika and oregano and cook for 5 minutes.

2 Add the beans, artichokes and tomatoes, stir to combine and bring to a simmer. Cook for a further 5 minutes or until the vegetable are just tender then transfer into a 30 x 18cm ovenproof dish.

3 Preheat the grill to medium.

4 Scatter the jalapeños, if using, and olives over the vegetables, then top with the tortilla chips and the grated cheese. Pop under the grill until the cheese is melted and slightly coloured, serve straight away with a dollop of sour cream and iceberg lettuce.

GOAT'S CHEESE OMELETTES WITH CHERRY TOMATO AND QUINCE

My jazzed-up cheese omelette is filled with tangy goat's cheese and **TOPPED WITH**

A SWEET TOMATO AND QUINCE DRESSING – the ultimate veggie omelette.

SERVES 4

4 tablespoons olive oil
1 red onion, finely chopped
1 tablespoon quince jelly
400g cherry tomatoes, halved
12 free-range eggs
1 tablespoon wholegrain mustard
50g butter
150g goat's cheese, crumbled
1 tablespoon chopped fresh basil leaves
crushed sea salt and freshly ground
   black pepper

1 Heat the oil in a medium saucepan over a medium heat, sauté the onion until tender, then add the quince jelly and cherry tomatoes. Cook until the jelly has melted and the tomatoes are warmed through. Remove from the heat and set aside.

2 Place the eggs, mustard and seasoning in a large jug, whisk well to combine. Preheat the oven to 150°C/300°F/gas mark 2.

3 Heat one-quarter of the butter in a large non-stick frying pan and pour in one-quarter of the egg mixture. Swirl the egg around the pan to evenly cover the base of the pan. Stir the mix with a fork until just set.

4 As soon as the omelette is set on the bottom, but still a little runny on the top, scatter over a quarter of the goat's cheese and season. Cook for a further 30 seconds. Fold the omelette in half and carefully slide it out onto a warm plate. Keep the omelette warm in the oven and repeat the process to make 3 more omelettes.

5 Add the basil to the sticky tomato and quince dressing, which can be served warm or at room temperature, and spoon over each omelette just before serving.

SUMMERTIME EGGS

This great one-pan brunch dish of summer **MEDITERRANEAN VEGETABLES**

with cracked pepper, eggs, fresh basil and extra virgin olive oil is a twist on the

Spanish classic, Flamenco Eggs. Serve with crusty baguette to mop up the egg yolks.

SERVES 4

300g new potatoes, scrubbed
   and cut into wedges
1 tablespoon olive oil
1 red onion, thinly sliced
2 garlic cloves, finely crushed
knob of unsalted butter
1 red pepper, deseeded and sliced
1 yellow pepper, deseeded and sliced
1 large courgette, sliced
5 large plum tomatoes, diced
1 tablespoon chopped fresh oregano
   leaves
4 large free-range eggs
extra virgin olive oil, for drizzling
crushed sea salt and cracked
   black peppercorns
torn fresh basil leaves, to garnish
baguette, to serve

1 Put the potato wedges in a saucepan of boiling salted water and cook for 5 minutes. Drain well and set aside on kitchen paper to dry.

2 Place a large non-stick frying pan to a medium heat, add the oil and fry the onion and garlic for 2 minutes. Add the potato wedges and butter, cook for a further 2 minutes, until all ingredients are slightly coloured. Add the peppers and courgette, cook until slightly softened, stirring occasionally. Add the tomatoes and oregano and season to taste.

3 Make 4 equal-sized holes in the vegetable mixture, big enough to crack an egg into. Carefully break an egg into each hole, lower the heat and cover with a lid. Cook for about 5 minutes or until the egg whites are just set. Then remove the lid and season well. Drizzle with extra virgin olive oil and scatter over the basil. Serve in the pan at the table with crusty baguette, and dig in!

HOT CHILLI CHICKPEAS

A SUPER-FAST STORECUPBOARD TREAT WITH A KICK – canned

chickpeas plus a few simple ingredients cooked together. This is usually made with

just lemon, olive oil and parsley, but I've jazzed it up with chilli and smoked paprika.

SERVES 4

2 tablespoons olive oil
1 medium onion, finely diced
2 garlic cloves, finely chopped
1 tablespoon smoked paprika
1 heaped teaspoon dried chilli flakes
zest and juice of 1 lemon
1 tablespoon cumin seeds
2 x 400g cans chickpeas, drained
2 tablespoons chopped fresh coriander
crushed sea salt and cracked
   black peppercorns

1 Heat the olive oil in a large, non-stick frying pan over a medium heat. Add the onion, garlic, paprika, chilli flakes, lemon zest and cumin seeds. Cook for 2 minutes, stirring occasionally.

2 Add the chickpeas and sauté for a further 2 minutes, stirring frequently. Stir in the lemon juice and coriander just before serving. Season to taste and serve.

MIXED BEAN RATATOUILLE

A hearty, baked ratatouille with a twist. I've used mixed pulses and fresh beans

to make this more substantial and turn it into a meal. Fantastic **SERVED WITH**

CHEESY GARLIC BREAD.

SERVES 4

2 tablespoons olive oil

2 shallots, diced

2 garlic cloves, finely chopped

1 tablespoon chopped fresh thyme
    leaves

1 tablespoon tomato purée

150g can cannellini beans, drained
    and rinsed

150g can borlotti beans, drained
    and rinsed

250g pack ready-to-eat Puy lentils

1 litre passata

200g green beans, topped

10 fresh basil leaves

crushed sea salt and freshly ground
    black pepper

garlic bread with melted cheese,
    to serve

1 Preheat the oven to 180°C/350°F/gas mark 4.

2 Heat the oil in a large saucepan and sauté the shallots, garlic and thyme for 4 minutes or until tender. Then add the tomato purée, cannellini beans, borlotti beans, lentils and passata, stir well. Transfer the mixture to a 2.5-litre casserole dish, cover with a lid and bake for 30 minutes, stirring after 15 minutes.

3 Put the green beans in a saucepan of lightly salted boiling water and cook for 4–5 minutes. Refresh under cold running water and drain well. Once cold, cut the beans in half.

4 Stir the green beans and basil into the ratatouille. Check the seasoning then serve with cheesy garlic bread.

RED FLANNEL HAZELNUT HASH

Red Flannel Hash is a New England speciality, made with potatoes, beetroot and corned beef. My version is a vibrant hash of diced **BEETROOT, SWEETCORN KERNELS** and **POTATOES** topped with crunchy cracked **HAZELNUTS**. Great as a side dish or as part of a mezze.

SERVES 4

450g potatoes, peeled and diced

2 tablespoons olive oil

1 small onion, diced

110g fresh or canned and drained sweetcorn kernels

2 garlic cloves, finely chopped

250g cooked beetroot, diced (1 small pack)

30g chopped fresh flat leaf parsley

30g toasted cracked hazelnuts

crushed sea salt and freshly ground black pepper

1 Blanch the diced potato in a saucepan of salted boiling water for 5 minutes, drain well and set aside.

2 Heat the oil in a large frying pan, add the onion, sweetcorn and potato and sauté for 3 minutes. Add the garlic and continue to cook for a further minute, then add the beetroot and warm through. Season and finish with fresh chopped parsley.

3 Arrange in a warm serving dish and sprinkle over the cracked hazelnuts.

DEVILLED MUSHROOMS ON TOAST

I've spiced up mushooms on toast with **PAPRIKA, CHILLI, WHOLEGRAIN MUSTARD** and **HONEY.** The spices really bring this dish to life and work brilliantly with **SWEET MANGO.**

SERVES 4

5 tablespoons olive oil
2 garlic cloves, finely chopped
8 large, flat mushrooms
15g butter
1 ripe mango, peeled and finely diced
¼ teaspoon dried chilli flakes
½ teaspoon smoked paprika
2 teaspoons wholegrain mustard
1 tablespoon clear blossom honey
4 thick slices brown bread
crushed sea salt and freshly ground
   black pepper
watercress or rocket, to serve

1 Preheat the oven to 150°C/300°F/gas mark 2.

2 Preheat a ridged griddle pan over a medium heat. Put the oil, garlic and mushrooms in a large bowl. Season well and toss the mushrooms to coat in the garlic oil. Cook the mushrooms in batches depending on the size of your griddle pan, for about 3 minutes on each side or until tender. Keep the mushrooms warm in the oven.

3 Melt the butter in a small saucepan over a medium heat. Add the mango and chilli flakes and cook for 2 minutes. Add the paprika, mustard and honey, stir well and cook over a medium heat until the mango starts to break up. Stir well to combine then remove from the heat and set aside.

4 Toast the bread on both sides and put 1 slice on 4 serving plates. Top each slice of toast with two mushrooms, drizzle over the mango sauce and serve with the watercress or rocket.

TURNIP GRATIN

A fantastic alternative to potato gratin, this filling dish **PUNCHES A GREAT**

FLAVOUR. At its best served in the colder winter months. This is great as a

vegetarian supper dish but the flavours also work brilliantly with lamb.

SERVES 4 AS A SIDE OR
2 AS A MAIN

4 or 5 small turnips, peeled
½ tablespoon salt
250ml whipping cream
knob of butter
leaves from 2 sprigs of fresh thyme
50g vegetarian Parmesan-style
   cheese, grated

1 Very thinly slice the turnips, ideally on a mandolin, put in a bowl and mix with the salt. Set aside for 10 minutes – the salt draws out any excess water from the turnips.

2 Preheat the grill to high

3 Place the cream, butter and thyme in a medium saucepan and gently heat to a simmer.

4 Remove the turnip slices from the bowl, rinse under cold running water and put them in a clean tea towel. Pat dry and then wring out to remove any excess water. Add the slices to the cream mixture. Simmer gently, stirring occasionally, until the turnip slices are tender and the cream has thickened.

5 Transfer the mixture to a 15 x 20cm ovenproof serving dish. Sprinkle the cheese over the top and place under the hot grill until golden brown and bubbling.

GARDEN PAN PIZZA

A scone-based pizza cooked in a frying pan **TOPPED WITH ARTICHOKES,**

OLIVES, TOMATOES, ASPARAGUS and finished off with mozzarella. The

scone-based dough is super quick and easy to make.

SERVES 4

4½ tablespoons olive oil
  plus extra for greasing

200g self-raising flour,
  plus extra for dusting

1 teaspoon salt

3 tablespoons sun-dried tomato purée

100ml cold water

125g asparagus tips

1 garlic clove, finely chopped

300g canned baby artichoke hearts,
  drained and halved

200g cherry tomatoes, halved

300g pitted black olives, drained

1 teaspoon dried parsley

1 teaspoon dried basil

1 teaspoon dried marjoram

125g bocconcini
  (mini mozzarella balls)

crushed sea salt and freshly ground
  black pepper

1 Preheat the oven to 200°C/400°F/gas mark 6. Oil a 28cm non-stick ovenproof frying pan or paella pan.

2 Put the flour, 2½ tablespoons of the oil, salt and tomato purée in a bowl. Add the water, a little at a time, to the flour and mix to form a soft, smooth dough. Add a little extra water if necessary.

3 Roll out the dough on a well-floured surface, to form a circle roughly the same size as the pan, then place it in the pan. Use your hand to stretch the dough to cover the base. Bake for about 5 minutes or until golden.

4 Cook the asparagus tips in a saucepan of boiling water for 3 minutes. Refresh under cold running water and drain well.

5 Combine the remaining oil, the garlic, artichokes, tomatoes, olives, herbs and asparagus tips. Mix to coat the vegetables in the garlic and herb oil and season well.

6 Spoon the vegetable mix over the pizza base, scatter it with the mozzarella balls and bake for 10 minutes or until the cheese has melted and vegetables are starting to colour.

7 Slide the pizza out of the pan onto a warmed serving plate and cut into 4.

GARDEN PAN PIZZA (Recipe on page 117)

SMOKED TOFU AND APRICOT BURGERS

Want a totally different veggie burger? Try these smoked tofu and apricot burgers –

A GREAT COMBINATION FOR A TASTY VEGETARIAN MAIN. Pop them on

the barbecue if you fancy. Serve in a bun with Zesty Poppyseed Coleslaw (see page 15).

SERVES 4

4 tablespoons soya or groundnut oil
1 red onion, roughly chopped
2 sticks celery, roughly chopped
2 garlic cloves, roughly chopped
110g dried apricots, roughly chopped
120g smoked tofu
60g fresh white breadcrumbs
1 free-range egg
1 teaspoon chopped fresh sage leaves
1 teaspoon chopped fresh thyme leaves
plain flour, for dusting
crushed sea salt and freshly ground
    black pepper
4 floured burger baps, to serve

1 Heat 2 tablespoons of the oil in a frying pan, over a medium heat. Add the onion, celery and garlic and cook for 4 minutes. Add the apricots and cook for a further 2 minutes. Remove from the heat and transfer everything to a food processor and wipe out the pan with kitchen paper.

2 Dry the tofu with kitchen paper and tear it into pieces. Add to the food processor and pulse to form a chunky paste. Season to taste.

3 Mix the breadcrumbs, egg, sage and thyme in a large bowl. Add the paste to the egg and herb breadcrumb mix and fold in until evenly combined.

4 Divide the mixture into 4 equal portions and, using floured hands, mould the mixture into burger shapes.

5 Heat the remaining oil in the frying pan over a high heat, add the burgers and cook for about 3 minutes on each side or until golden all over. Serve in floured burger baps.

NUT KOFTAS

Middle Eastern koftas are traditionally made with lamb or beef, but my modern

version used beans, mixed nuts, spices and herbs for a completely new angle.

These are **SERVED WITH A HERBY YOGURT DIP** and grilled pittas.

SERVES 4

For the koftas

4 tablespoons olive oil

2 shallots, diced

2 garlic cloves, crushed

½ teaspoon chilli powder

1 tablespoon curry paste

2 tablespoons crunchy
  peanut butter

60g roasted salted almonds

175g ground almonds

400g can cannellini beans,
  drained and rinsed

1 free-range egg

plain flour, for dusting

crushed sea salt and freshly ground
  black pepper

4 wamed pitta breads, to serve

For the yogurt dip

juice of 1 lime

200g natural yogurt

1 tablespoon chopped fresh
  mint leaves

1 tablespoon chopped fresh
  coriander leaves

1 Soak 8 wooden skewers in cold water for 20 minutes (this prevents them from burning).

2 To make the dip, put the lime juice, yogurt, mint and coriander in a bowl, stir well and season to taste. Cover and set aside until ready to serve.

3 Heat two tablespoons of the oil in a small frying pan over a medium heat, add the shallots and cook for 4 minutes. Now add the garlic, chilli powder and curry paste, cook for a further 2 minutes. Transfer the mixture to a food processor. Add the peanut butter, the roasted and ground almonds and the beans, blend for about 2 minutes then season to taste. Add the egg and blend to form a thick paste.

4 Preheat the grill to medium. Line the grill tray with kitchen foil.

5 Using floured hands, divide the mixture into 8 equal portions and mould each onto a skewer, forming a sausage shape. Place the skewers onto the lined tray and brush with 1 tablespoon of the olive oil. Grill for about 5 minutes or until golden, turning during cooking.

6 Place the koftas on a warmed serving plate and drizzle over the remaining oil. Serve with the yogurt dip and warmed pittas.

SMOKED TOFU SATAY KEBABS

I've used smoked tofu here instead of the more usual chicken. Big on flavour, this crunchy **PEANUT BUTTER-BASED SAUCE** also works well with vegetables, fish or meats.

SERVES 4

For the kebabs

5 tablespoons crunchy peanut butter
½ teaspoon dried chilli flakes
   (more if you like it hot!)
2 teaspoons maple syrup
1 teaspoon rice wine vinegar
1 teaspoon dark soy sauce
1 garlic clove, finely chopped
zest and juice of 1 lime
5 tablespoons coconut milk
400g smoked tofu,
   cut into large cubes
1 red onion, cut into wedges
1 aubergine, cubed

For the salad

½ cucumber
250g beansprouts
1 tablespoon toasted sesame seeds
juice of 1 lemon
1 teaspoon extra virgin olive oil
crushed sea salt and freshly ground
   black pepper

1 Soak 12 wooden skewers in cold water for 20 minutes (this prevents them from burning). Preheat the grill to medium.

2 Put the peanut butter, chilli flakes, maple syrup, vinegar, soy sauce, garlic, lime zest and juice and coconut milk in a food processor, blitz to a thick smooth paste then set aside.

3 Thread alternate pieces of tofu, onion and aubergine onto the soaked wooden skewers.

4 Brush the peanut paste on the kebabs. Grill the kebabs, turning them occasionally, for around 12 minutes, brushing on more peanut paste as they cook.

5 Meanwhile, remove the skin of the cucumber using a vegetable peeler, then continue to peel ribbons of cucumber into a bowl, peeling as far as the seed, discard the core. Add the beansprouts, sesame seeds, lemon juice and extra virgin olive oil to the bowl, season and mix. Pile the salad on a serving plate. Warm up any leftover peanut sauce in a small saucepan.

6 Lay the tofu kebabs on top of the salad and serve drizzled with the sauce and any cooking juices.

SWEETCORN, MASCARPONE AND HAZELNUT RISOTTO

Instead of Parmesan, this fresh sweetcorn risotto is bound with **RICH, CREAMY MASCARPONE CHEESE** and finished with **TOASTED HAZELNUTS.** Brilliant flavour combinations.

SERVES 4

2 corn on the cob
2 tablespoons olive oil
1 onion, finely chopped
500ml water
2 garlic cloves, finely chopped
300g Arborio risotto rice
170ml dry white wine
150g mascarpone cheese
extra virgin olive oil, to drizzle (optional)
crushed sea salt and freshly ground
   black pepper
6 toasted hazelnuts, chopped or grated,
   to serve

1 Slice the corn kernels from the cobs, set the kernels aside. Cut the cobs into large chunks. Heat 1 tablespoon of the oil in a saucepan over a medium heat, add half the onion and the corn cob pieces. Cook for 2 minutes then add the water, bring to a gentle simmer and cook for about 10 minutes.

2 Place a medium non-stick saucepan over a medium heat, add the remaining oil and sauté the garlic and remaining onion for 1 minute. Add the rice and stir to coat the grains all over, then add the wine and simmer until it reduces by half.

3 Strain the hot stock into a measuring jug. Gradually add up to 300ml of the stock into the rice pan, stirring in each addition, before adding the next, until the rice is cooked through – this will take about 12 minutes.

4 Put a ladleful of the remaining hot stock and half the corn kernels in a food processor and blend until smooth. Pass the blended mixture through a fine sieve, and add to the risotto.

5 Add the remaining corn kernels to the risotto, heat through and fold in the mascarpone. Season to taste.

6 Loosen the mixture with the remaining hot corn stock if required. Serve in warmed bowls with a drizzle of extra virgin olive oil and a sprinkling of hazelnuts.

VEGETABLE PAELLA

A simple, one-pan **MEDITERRANEAN-STYLE RECIPE** with brown rice, mixed vegetables and smoked tofu. A flavoursome vegetarian twist on the traditional seafood paella.

SERVES 4

2 tablespoons olive oil
2 banana shallots, chopped
2 cloves garlic, finely chopped
1 aubergine, diced
1 red pepper, deseeded and diced
150g fresh sweetcorn kernels
200g long grain brown rice
1.2 litres hot good vegetable stock
150g chestnut mushrooms, quartered
1 large courgette, diced
380g can artichoke hearts, drained
   and halved
200g smoked tofu, diced
3 tablespoons chopped fresh basil
½ lemon
crushed sea salt and freshly ground
   black pepper

1 Place a large heavy-based frying pan or paella pan over a medium heat, add the oil and sauté the shallots and garlic for 2 minutes. Add the aubergine, stirring occasionally, and cook for about 5 minutes until the aubergine starts to colour. Stir in the pepper and sweetcorn then add the rice and combine with the vegetables.

2 Add 500ml of the hot stock, bring to a simmer and cover with a loosely fitted piece of kitchen foil. Cook for 20 minutes. Add a further 500ml of stock, the mushrooms and courgettes and cook for a further 20 minutes, stirring occasionally.

3 Check the rice is just tender, then add the artichokes and tofu, stir well and heat through for 2 minutes. Add any remaining stock to loosen the mixture.

4 To serve, stir in the chopped basil, squeeze over a little lemon juice and season to taste.

AUBERGINE, MOZZARELLA AND ONION TRAY BAKE

A hearty meat-free alternative using layers of fried aubergines, onion relish, tomatoes and mozzarella, **TOPPED WITH CRISPY PARMESAN BREADCRUMBS.** This is my veggie spin on Chicken Parmigiana. The shallots add sweetness while the cinnamon brings out the flavours.

SERVES 4

2 large aubergines

4 tablespoons olive oil

3 banana shallots, diced

2 garlic cloves, finely chopped

1 tablespoon tomato purée

3 tablespoons sherry vinegar

2 x 400g cans whole plum tomatoes, drained

½ cinnamon stick

leaves from 4 sprigs of fresh thyme

4 tablespoons onion relish

3 x 150g balls mozzarella cheese, sliced

12 basil leaves

30g panko breadcrumbs

100g vegetarian Parmesan-style cheese, grated

crushed sea salt and cracked black peppercorns

1 Preheat the oven to 180°C/350°F/gas mark 4.

2 Cut the aubergines into 1cm thick slices and brush both sides with 3 tablespoons of the oil and season. Heat a ridged griddle pan or non-stick frying pan over a medium heat and cook the aubergine slices until slightly coloured and tender, turning occasionally. Transfer to kitchen paper to drain, and set aside.

3 Heat a large saucepan over a medium heat, add 1 tablespoon of the oil and add the shallots, cook, stirring for 2 minutes. Add the garlic and tomato purée, stir and cook for a further 2 minutes. Stir in the vinegar and cook for 1 minute. Crush the drained tomatoes with a spoon and combine with the mixture. Add the cinnamon stick and thyme leaves, lower the heat and cook for 10 minutes, stirring occasionally, until thickened.

4 Spoon a layer of tomato sauce into a 30 x 20cm ovenproof dish. Cover with a layer of aubergines and 1 tablespoon of the onion relish. Add a layer of sliced mozzarella, some ripped basil leaves and cracked black pepper. Repeat the layers, finishing with a layer of tomato sauce. Mix together the breadcrumbs and cheese and scatter over the top.

5 Bake for 30 minutes until golden and bubbling. Remove from the oven and leave to stand for 5 minutes before serving, then dig in!

SAVOURY SUMMER PUDDING

This really speaks for itself. A savoury version of the dessert classic **WITH FRESH**

SUMMER FLAVOURS in every slice. Full of delicious Mediterranean vegetables.

SERVES 6

2 tablespoons olive oil

1 small yellow courgette,
cut into 2cm dice

1 small green courgette,
cut into 2cm dice

1 dessertspoon dried herbes
de Provence

500g passata

2 x 400g loaves of focaccia, crusts
removed, cut into 1cm slices

100g baby plum tomatoes, halved

50g black pitted niçoise olives

50g sun-blush tomatoes

280g jar antipasto baby artichokes in oil,
drained and quartered

3 spring onions, sliced

1 tablespoon extra virgin olive oil

crushed sea salt and cracked
black pepper

fresh basil leaves, to garnish

1 Brush a 1.5 litre pudding basin with 1 tablespoon of the oil, line with 2 layers of clingfilm leaving enough overhanging the rim of the basin to wrap up and cover the finished pudding.

2 Heat the remaining oil in a frying pan and sauté the courgettes with the herbes de Provence for 2 minutes until slightly softened then drain and cool on kitchen paper.

3 Pour the passata into a bowl and season to taste. Cut a rough circle of focaccia to fit the bottom of the lined pudding basin and dip the bread circle in the passata. Place the bread circle in the base of the lined pudding bowl and repeat the process using the remaining sliced bread to line the sides of the basin, leaving any excess overhanging to cover the top of your pudding.

4 Mix the remaining ingredients, except the extra virgin olive oil and basil leaves, with the remaining passata. Pour the vegetable and passata mixture into the bread-lined basin. Cover the ingredients with any overhanging bread. Wrap up the pudding with the overhanging clingfilm, cover with a small plate and top with a weight. Chill in the fridge overnight.

5 To serve, carefully open up the clingfilm and invert the basin onto a serving plate. Remove the basin and peel off the clingfilm. Drizzle with extra virgin olive oil and garnish with basil leaves. Serve cut into wedges either on its own or as part of a picnic-style buffet.

CHESTNUT, CHEDDAR AND SAGE RICE CAKE

A world away from shop-bought puffed rice cakes, this is a rich, savoury, gooey rice cake

WITH AROMATIC SAGE and a **SWEET CRANBERRY SAUCE**. I've included the classic

combination of apple and cheese – it's like a Ploughman's with rice!

SERVES 6

250g long-grain brown rice

2 tablespoons olive oil, plus extra
    for greasing

2 red onions, thinly sliced

2 sticks celery, sliced

2 garlic cloves, sliced

1 leek, sliced

1 large Bramley apple, peeled and
    grated

200g pack cooked and peeled whole
    chestnuts, sliced

80g mature Cheddar cheese, grated

1 free-range egg

2 tablespoons chopped fresh
    sage leaves

Worcestershire sauce, to taste

5 tablespoons cranberry sauce

crushed sea salt and freshly ground
    black pepper

1 Tip the rice into a large saucepan of boiling water and cook according to the packet instructions until just tender – this will take around 20 minutes. Drain, rinse under cold running water and set aside.

2 Preheat the oven to 180°C/350°F/gas mark 4 and brush a 20cm springform cake tin with oil.

3 Heat the oil in a large non-stick frying pan over a medium heat and add the onions, celery and garlic, cook for 5 minutes to soften then add the leek and apple. Cook for a further 2 minutes then stir in the chestnuts. Add the cooked vegetables to the cooked rice in the pan and stir well. Mix in the cheese, egg and sage, add a good dash of Worcestershire sauce and season to taste.

4 Spoon the mixture into the cake tin and flatten the top with the back of a spoon. Bake for 20 minutes until lightly browned. Remove and leave in the tin for 5 minutes.

5 Heat the cranberry sauce with 1 tablespoon water in a small saucepan, over a medium heat and stir well to combine. Remove the cake from the tin, cut into wedges and serve with the warm cranberry sauce. You could also eat the cake cold, if you wish.

GORGONZOLA MACARONI

Macaroni cheese with a **CREAMY, TANGY BLUE CHEESE SAUCE** – I like it with veggie bacon but it's entirely optional. The **CRISPY BREADCRUMB TOPPING** adds a nice contrasting texture.

I use single cream here rather than double because the cheese is so rich.

SERVES 4

2 tablespoons olive oil

1 onion, finely diced

2 garlic cloves, finely chopped

150g Quorn bacon style slices (optional), chopped into lardons

200ml semi-skimmed milk

200ml single cream

125g Gorgonzola cheese (or Dolcelatte for a vegetarian alternative)

300g dried macaroni

2 tablespoons chopped fresh sage leaves

100g Cheddar cheese, grated

50g fresh white breadcrumbs

freshly ground black pepper

1 Preheat the oven to 230°C/450°F/gas mark 8.

2 Heat the oil in a large frying pan over a medium heat, add the onion, garlic and bacon (if using) and cook for 5 minutes. Pour in the milk and cream and bring to boiling point then add the Gorgonzola and season with pepper to taste.

3 Meanwhile, cook the macaroni, bring a large pan of salted water to the boil, add the pasta and cook according to the packet instructions (about 10 minutes). Drain the pasta, add the sage and cheese sauce, stir then transfer to a 28 x 15cm baking dish.

4 Mix together the Cheddar cheese and breadcrumbs and sprinkle over the pasta and bake for 10 minutes or until golden brown.

CARROT AND CREAM CHEESE TART

Carrot tarts, both sweet and savoury, were very popular during the Elizabethan times. This is my modern-day version, inspired by two popular flavour combinations: carrot and coriander, and carrot and orange. Creamy **SWEET CARROT** filling in oaty pastry **TOPPED WITH CORIANDER.**

SERVES 4

For the pastry

150g plain flour, plus extra for dusting
50g porridge oats
80g unsalted butter, cubed and chilled
3 tablespoons iced water

For the filling

500g carrots, peeled and sliced
1 teaspoon coriander seeds, crushed
80g full-fat cream cheese
zest of 1 orange
1 large free-range egg, beaten
2 tablespoons chopped fresh coriander
crushed sea salt and freshly ground
    black pepper
green salad, to serve

1 Combine the flour and oats with a pinch of salt in a mixing bowl. Rub in the butter, and gradually stir in enough of the iced water to form a soft dough. Wrap in clingfilm and chill in the fridge for 30 minutes.

2 Preheat the oven to 180°C/350°F/gas mark 4.

3 Roll out the pastry on a lightly floured worksurface to a circle large enough to line a 20cm loose-based tart tin. Line the tin with the pastry and trim off any excess. Prick the pastry base with a fork, line with baking parchment and fill with baking beans. Bake blind for 20 minutes. Remove from the oven, take out the baking parchment and beans and set the tart shell aside.

4 Put the carrots and coriander seeds in a medium saucepan, cover with cold water and add a pinch of salt. Bring to a simmer and cook until just tender – about 8–10 minutes. Drain well and blitz to a purée in a blender. Add the cheese, orange zest and egg and blitz again. Transfer to a bowl and stir in the chopped coriander leaves, season to taste.

5 Spoon the carrot filling into the pastry case and bake for 15–20 minutes or until just set. Remove and allow to cool slightly on a wire rack. Serve with a simple green salad.

DESSERTS

PEAR AND SZECHUAN PEPPER TARTE TATIN

Pears coated in a **FIERY PEPPER CARAMEL** and baked on a puff pastry base

make a great pud for cooler autumn days. The aromats bring the caramel to life and

work wonderfully with the pears.

SERVES 6

60g unsalted butter

75g caster sugar

4–5 Williams pears, peeled,
  halved and cored

½ cinnamon stick

1 star anise

1 vanilla pod, split

1 teaspoon szechuan
  peppercorns, cracked

200g sheet ready-rolled puff pastry

whipped cream or vanilla ice cream,
  to serve

1 Preheat the oven to 200°C/400°F/gas mark 6.

2 Melt the butter in a 24cm non-stick ovenproof frying pan, add
the sugar and cook over a medium heat until golden brown. Add the
pear halves to the pan in a circle cut-side up, placing one pear half
in the centre, and coat in the caramel. Now add the cinnamon stick,
star anise, vanilla pod and szechuan pepper to the pan.

3 Unroll the pastry and cut out a 24cm circle. Prick the pastry with
a fork and pierce a hole in the middle. Place the puff pastry round
on top of the frying pan and tuck the edges in and around the pears.

4 Bake for 15–20 minutes or until the pastry is golden brown.

5 Remove from the oven and allow the tatin to rest for a couple of
minutes. Place a large serving plate over the pan and, holding plate
and pan with oven gloves, carefully (the caramel will be very hot)
and quickly invert them together, so that the tatin ends up pastry
case down on the plate. Remove the cinnamon stick, star anise and
vanilla pod before you cut the tart into portions.

6 Serve with whipped cream or vanilla ice cream.

QUICK RASPBERRY SHORTBREAD MESS

A **QUICK AND EASY UPDATE ON THE SUMMER CLASSIC** Eton mess –

with raspberries, mint and shortbread biscuits. I've used fromage frais instead of

cream, making the dessert lighter and slightly more guilt-free.

SERVES 4

8 shortbread biscuits
2 meringue nests
seeds from 1 vanilla pod
400g fromage frais
2 teaspoons icing sugar
300g raspberries
4 fresh mint leaves, chopped
4 sprigs of mint, to decorate

1 Roughly break up the biscuits and meringue nests.

2 To remove the seeds from the vanilla pod, cut the pod lengthways with a small sharp knife. Use the tip of the knife to scrape out the seeds.

3 Mix together the fromage frais, vanilla seeds and icing sugar in a large bowl until smooth then fold in the shortbread, meringue, all but 4 of the raspberries, and the chopped mint leaves.

2 Spoon the mess into 4 glasses and serve decorated with a raspberry and sprig of mint.

STRAWBERRY AND CREAM BREAD AND BUTTER PUDDING

The ultimate nursery pud just got better – **BREAD AND BUTTER** pudding with

strawberry jam and cream, plus some pistachios for extra crunch. A classic in a

classic. This is a perfect summer dessert, and the colours are brilliant.

SERVES 4–6

40g unsalted butter, at room
   temperature plus extra for greasing
8 slices of stale bread, crusts removed
40g strawberry jam
40g pistachio nuts, chopped
3 large free-range eggs
50g caster sugar
seeds from 1 vanilla pod
200ml double cream
200ml whole milk
15g light brown sugar
clotted cream or ice cream, to serve

1 Preheat the oven to 180°C/350°F/gas mark 4. Butter a 26 x 18cm baking dish.

2 To remove the seeds from the vanilla pod, cut the pod lengthways with a small sharp knife. Use the tip of the knife to scrape out the seeds.

3 Make 4 jam sandwiches with the bread, butter and jam. Cut each sandwich into 4 triangles.

4 Arrange the sandwiches, points upwards, in the buttered dish, sprinkle half the pistachios between them.

5 Whisk together the eggs, sugar and vanilla seeds in a large jug then add the cream and milk and whisk again. Pour over the bread and leave to soak for around 20 minutes, pressing the triangles down slightly at the top so the egg mix covers everything.

6 Sprinkle over the remaining pistachios and the brown sugar. Bake for 30–40 minutes, or until the pudding is set and has a golden crust.

7 Serve with clotted cream or ice cream.

VANILLA ORANGE CINNAMON COUSCOUS

Couscous is more usually found in savoury dishes, but it also **WORKS**

BRILLIANTLY in this milk-based rice pudding alternative. It is flavoured

with cinnamon, orange **AND A DOLLOP OF CREAM**.

SERVES 4

300ml whole milk
pinch of salt
2 tablespoons demerara sugar
½ teaspoon ground cinnamon
1 orange, zest, juice and segmented
½ vanilla pod
150g couscous
150ml whipping cream
3 fresh mint leaves, shredded
1 tablespoon clear blossom honey

1 Put the milk, salt, sugar, cinnamon, orange zest and juice in a medium saucepan. Scrape the seeds from the vanilla pod and add them, with the pod, to the pan, and bring to a simmer over a medium heat.

2 Put the couscous in a mixing bowl and pour over the simmered milk mixture, cover with clingfilm and leave to stand for 5 minutes.

3 Whip the cream to form soft peaks and set aside. Uncover the couscous, remove the vanilla pod and use a fork to fluff up the couscous grains. Stir in half the cream and half the mint.

4 Divide the mixture and the orange segments between 4 glasses. Top with a dollop of the remaining cream, a drizzle of honey and the remaining shredded mint.

BANOFFEE SOUFFLÉS

I like to think of this as banoffee pie deconstructed. It's a very moreish soufflé with a

BANANA AND TOFFEE MIX and a sprinkling of digestive biscuit crumbs. A true piece

of banoffee heaven! Drizzle with dark chocolate sauce or serve with a dollop of ice cream.

SERVES 4

1 x 175g can condensed milk
3 large ripe bananas
150ml whole milk
4 free-range eggs, separated
65g caster sugar, plus 4 tablespoons for
    dusting
30g plain flour, sifted
butter, at room temperature, for greasing
2 digestive biscuits, crushed

1 Place the unopened can of condensed milk in a small saucepan, cover with water and bring to the boil. Simmer for 3 hours, making sure the can is always covered with water. Remove and allow the tin to cool.

2 Peel the bananas and whiz them in a food processor to form a smooth purée.

3 Warm the whole milk in a second small pan, then stir in the banana purée.

4 Whisk together the egg yolks and sugar in a large bowl, add the flour and whisk to form a smooth paste.

5 Add the banana and milk mixture to the paste and mix well. Return everything to the saucepan and gently heat, stirring until thickened, then pour into a clean bowl, cover with clingfilm and leave to cool.

6 Preheat the oven to 200°C/400°F/gas mark 6.

7 Butter 4 150ml ramekins. Add 1 tablespoon of sugar to each ramekin and tilt and rotate, coating the inside with sugar. Chill the ramekins in the fridge.

8 Whisk the egg whites until they form stiff peaks.

9 Whisk 250g of the cooled banana mixture with 125g of the cooled condensed milk (it will resemble caramel). Add half the egg whites and whisk, then fold in the remaining whites with a metal spoon. Be careful not to knock the air out.

10 Spoon the soufflé mixture into the ramekins, carefully tap the dishes on the work surface (this releases any trapped air pockets), smooth over with a palette knife and sprinkle with crushed digestives.

11 Place on a baking tray and bake for 10–15 minutes.

12 Serve the soufflés immediately.

BANANA PANCAKES WITH MAPLE SYRUP AND PECAN NUT BUTTER

This is my twist on the American brunch favourite of pancakes with maple syrup.

Here, thick American-style **PANCAKES MADE WITH CRUSHED BANANAS** are

served with maple syrup and pecan butter. Perfect for a special occasion.

SERVES 4

For the butter

130g butter, at room temperature
1 tablespoon icing sugar, sifted
1 tablespoon maple syrup
1 tablespoon pecan nuts, finely chopped

For the pancakes

2 soft bananas
seeds from 1 vanilla pod (optional)
150g self-raising flour
1 teaspoon baking powder
1 tablespoon caster sugar
1 free-range egg
75ml whole milk
3 tablespoons vegetable oil, for cooking

1 Preheat the oven to 180°C/350°F/gas mark 4.

2 To make the maple syrup and pecan nut butter, in a bowl beat together the butter and icing sugar until smooth. Add the maple syrup, stir well and then fold in the pecan nuts. Set aside until ready to serve.

3 Mash the bananas with the vanilla seeds until smooth. Sift the flour and baking powder into a mixing bowl.

4 Whisk together the caster sugar and egg then stir in the milk. Add the egg mixture to the dry ingredients and stir until smooth. Fold in the bananas.

5 Heat 1 tablespoon of the oil in a large non-stick frying pan over a medium heat. Drop 4 tablespoonfuls of batter into the pan, spaced well apart, and cook for 2 minutes or until bubbles form on the surface, then flip and cook for a further 2 minutes on the other side. Remove from the pan and repeat to make 12 pancakes.

6 Place the pancakes on a non-stick baking tray and warm through in the oven for 4 minutes. Serve the pancakes hot with the maple syrup and pecan nut butter.

APPLE AND RAISIN SAMOSAS WITH STEM GINGER AND ICE CREAM

Samosas are traditionally a savoury appetiser, so this sweet version is something totally different.

Chunky stewed apple, raisin and cinnamon compote bound in filo pastry, **DEEP FRIED** and

SERVED WITH VANILLA ICE CREAM and stem ginger. I love the combination of hot and cold.

SERVES 4

8 large Bramley apples, peeled, cored and diced

½ teaspoon ground cinnamon

1 cinnamon stick

2 tablespoons sugar

seeds from 1 vanilla pod

100g raisins

12 30 x 18cm filo pastry sheets

600ml oil, for deep frying

1 litre vanilla ice cream

4 stem ginger balls in syrup, drained and finely diced

2 tablespoons stem ginger syrup (from the jar)

1 Preheat the oven to 180°C/350°F/gas mark 4.

2 Place the diced apples, ground cinnamon, cinnamon stick, sugar, vanilla seeds and raisins in a saucepan over a medium heat, simmer until the apples are tender and the mixture thickens. Remove the cinnamon stick and set aside to cool.

3 Fold each filo pastry sheet in half lengthways, spoon 2 tablespoons of compote at one end of the pastry sheet, in the corner. Brush a little water around the compote, then fold this corner over to the long side to make a triangle. Pat down the edges to make a seal, lightly brush the remaining pastry with water. Continue folding the triangle along the length of the pastry until all the pastry is used up to make a neat triangular samosa. Repeat the process to make 12 samosas in total.

4 Heat the oil to 180°C in a medium, heavy-based saucepan. Cook the samosas, 3 at a time, for about 3 minutes or until golden brown. Transfer the cooked samosas to a non-stick baking tray and keep warm in the oven while cooking the remaining batches.

5 Serve the samosas with a scoop of vanilla ice cream, sprinkled with diced ginger and a drizzle of ginger syrup.

JASMINE RICE PUDDING WITH APRICOTS, CARAMEL AND ALMONDS

A CREAMY, VELVETY PUDDING made with jasmine rice instead of traditional

pudding rice and served with deliciously sticky caramelised apricots. The flaked

almonds add some extra crunch.

SERVES 4

150g jasmine rice
pinch of salt
500ml whole milk
2 jasmine teabags
300ml whipping cream
100g caster sugar, plus 1 tablespoon
½ vanilla pod
4 firm apricots, halved and stoned
knob of unsalted butter
toasted flaked almonds, to decorate

1 Put 250ml water, rice and salt in a medium saucepan, bring to a gentle simmer, cover with a lid and cook for 10 minutes.

2 Pour the milk into a separate pan, add the teabags and bring to a simmer. Remove from the heat and set aside to infuse for about 6 minutes. Discard the teabags.

3 Add the infused milk, 250ml of the cream and 100g of sugar to the rice. Scrape the seeds from the vanilla pod and add them, with the pod, to the rice. Cook the rice for about 30 minutes, uncovered, over a medium heat, stirring occasionally, until tender and the mixture has thickened slightly.

4 Heat a non-stick frying pan over a medium heat and scatter over the 1 tablespoon sugar. Lay the apricot halves, flat side down, in the pan, being careful of the hot sugar as it will be starting to melt and turn amber in colour. When the sugar is amber coloured, add the butter to the pan and roll the apricot halves around in the hot caramel. Lower the heat and add the remaining cream, simmer for about 5 minutes until the apricots have slightly softened and the caramel has dissolved into the cream. Remove the pan from the heat and allow the apricots to cool slightly.

5 To serve, remove the vanilla pod from the rice mixture and discard. Spoon the mix into serving bowls, top with caramelised apricots and a drizzle of sauce then scatter over a few toasted flaked almonds.

MELON AND GINGER SOUP

This is soup, but not as you know it. A sweet, chilled soup served with gingerbread

croûtons and **A DRIZZLE OF CRÈME FRAÎCHE** – a perfect refreshing finish

to a meal on a hot day.

SERVES 4

50ml orange juice

1 small stem ginger ball in syrup, drained and roughly chopped

1 star anise

1.5kg honeydew melon, peeled, deseeded and roughly diced

1 tablespoon clear blossom honey

1 tablespoon lime juice

60g ginger cake, cut into 1cm dice

80g crème fraîche

1 Put 50ml water in a saucepan with the orange juice, chopped ginger and star anise and bring to the boil. Remove the star anise and set aside to cool.

2 Cut a small amount of the roughly diced melon into fine dice and reserve for decorating.

3 Place the remaining melon, honey, lime juice and the orange and ginger stock into a blender, whiz until smooth and pass through a fine sieve. Chill for 1 hour.

4 Preheat the oven to 180°C/350°F/gas mark 4.

5 Spread out the ginger cake dice on a non-stick baking tray and bake for 5–10 minutes or until lightly crisp.

6 Serve the melon soup in chilled bowls, decorated with reserved melon dice, the ginger croûtons and a drizzle of crème fraîche.

MICROWAVE STICKY ORANGE PUDDING

Classic steamed sponge puddings can take over 2 hours to cook. Why wait? This dessert is **MIXED THEN COOKED AND READY IN JUST 15 MINUTES** – perfect almost-instant comfort food on a cold winter's night.

SERVES 4

120g butter, at room temperature,
  plus extra for greasing

2 tablespoons golden syrup

1 orange

110g caster sugar

2 free-range eggs

180g self-raising flour

1 tablespoon warm water

vanilla custard, cream or ice cream,
  to serve

1 Butter a 1.5 litre glass bowl and spoon in the golden syrup.

2 Zest the orange and place the zest in a mixing bowl. Remove the rind from the orange and segment, reserving any juice. Add the juice to the bowl with the zest. Loosely arrange the orange segments in the bowl with the syrup.

3 Put the butter and sugar into the mixing bowl with the orange zest and juice and beat until light and fluffy. Then beat in the eggs, one at a time, with a little flour. Fold in the remaining flour and warm water to make the mixture a smooth dropping consistency.

4 Scrape the mixture into the glass bowl over the orange segments, cover with clingfilm and microwave on high (800 watt) for about 6 minutes. Adjust the cooking time depending on the microwave wattage.

5 Leave to stand for 2–3 minutes and then turn out onto a warmed serving plate, and dig in! A slice goes well with vanilla custard, cream or ice cream.

ORANGE AND ALMOND POLENTA CAKE

A gluten-free fruit and nut cake packed with honeyed raisins and **TOPPED WITH**

GLACÉ ICING. Polenta isn't often found in sweet dishes, but it adds lightness to this

cake and creates a real treat for people on a gluten-free diet.

SERVES 4–6

270ml olive oil, plus extra for greasing
4 tablespoons clear blossom honey
170g raisins
370g caster sugar
zest and juice of 1 orange
185g ground almonds
180g fine polenta
2 teaspoons gluten-free baking powder
200g icing sugar
3–4 teaspoons boiling water

1 Preheat the oven to 180°C/350°F/gas mark 4. Grease and line a 20cm springform or loose-based cake round/square tin with baking parchment.

2 Put the honey and raisins in a small saucepan, heat gently until the honey melts. Stir well and set aside to cool.

3 Whisk together the oil, sugar, orange zest and juice in a large mixing bowl. Add the honeyed raisins. Once combined, add the almonds, polenta and baking powder and whisk again until all the ingredients are well incorporated.

4 Pour the mixture into the prepared tin. Bake for 1 hour, or until the cake is cooked but still moist. To test, insert a skewer or cocktail stick into the cake and if it comes out just clean then the cake is ready. Leave the cake in its tin on a wire rack to cool for about 20 minutes.

5 When the cake has almost cooled, remove from the tin. Sift the icing sugar into a bowl and gradually stir in enough boiling water to make a thick icing; the icing should leave a trail when you lift the spoon out of the bowl. Spoon this over the cake and leave to set for 20 minutes before serving.

GINGER CAKE WITH ROSÉ WINE STRAWBERRIES

A LIGHT GINGERBREAD CAKE sandwiched together with cream and strawberries in **ROSÉ WINE**.

This is a real summer treat – rosé wine always make me think of sunny afternoons, and the strawberries

soak up the flavour brilliantly. It's like a gingerbread Victoria Sandwich!

SERVES 8

For the syrup

2 tablespoons seedless strawberry jam
1 teaspoon caster sugar
1 vanilla pod, halved
250ml rosé wine

For the cake

250g unsalted butter, plus extra for
   greasing
250g soft brown sugar
2 small free-range eggs
6 tablespoons black treacle, warmed
1½ teaspoons ground ginger
1½ teaspoons mixed spice
500g plain flour
85g ground almonds
85g raisins
85g sultanas
1½ teaspoons bicarbonate of soda
200ml strong ale (I use Tribute Ale)

For the filling

350ml whipping cream
250g strawberries, hulled and halved
6 fresh mint leaves, roughly torn
icing sugar, for dusting

1 Preheat the oven to 180°C/350°F/gas mark 4. Grease and line a 20 x 30cm cake tin with baking parchment.

2 Put all the syrup ingredients in a saucepan, bring to the boil then simmer until reduced by one-third. Set aside to cool.

3 Cream together the butter and sugar in a large mixing bowl, and gradually beat in the eggs. Beat in the warmed treacle, then stir in the spices, flour, almonds and dried fruit. Mix the bicarbonate of soda into the beer and fold into the cake mix.

4 Pour the cake mixture into the prepared tin and bake for about 30 minutes. To test if the cake is cooked, pierce with a small knife, and if the end comes out clean the cake is ready. Leave to cool in its tin on a wire rack.

5 Whip the cream to soft peaks. Slice the cake in half lengthways and place one layer on a serving plate, drizzle over some of the cooled strawberry syrup and spread over half the whipped cream. Top with the halved strawberries, torn mint and remaining cream and syrup. Add the top layer of cake, dust with sifted icing sugar and serve.

SOFT MERINGUE AND LEMON CURD ROLL WITH STRAWBERRY DAIQUIRI SAUCE

I love sipping a strawberry daiquiri when relaxing on a golden beach on holiday. Here, the main ingredients of a daiquiri make a great sauce **DRIZZLED OVER GOOEY, LEMON CURD-FILLED MERINGUE ROLL**. The sauce is also fantastic with crushed ice as a drink or drizzled over a scoop of sorbet.

SERVES 4

For the sauce

280g strawberries, hulled and halved
3 tablespoons white rum
30g icing sugar
4 teaspoons lime juice

For the meringue roll

4 free-range egg whites
190g caster sugar
250ml double cream
seeds from ½ vanilla pod
2 tablespoons lemon curd
sifted icing sugar and fresh mint leaves, to decorate

1 Preheat the oven to 180°C/350°F/gas mark 4. Line a 23 x 30cm Swiss roll tin with baking parchment.

2 To make the sauce, blitz all the ingredients together in a blender. Chill until ready to serve.

3 Put the eggs whites in a bowl and whisk until stiff. Slowly add the sugar, 1 tablespoon at a time, whisking between each addition, until stiff and glossy. Spoon the mixture evenly into the lined tin. Bake for 15 minutes, until crisp on the outside.

4 Remove the tin from the oven and lay a sheet of baking parchment on the work surface. Turn out the meringue onto the sheet and peel off the baking parchment then leave to cool.

5 Pour the cream into a mixing bowl and scrape the seeds from the vanilla pod into it. Whip until the cream forms soft peaks. Whisk in the lemon curd and spoon the cream mixture over the meringue. Immediately roll the meringue up, as you would a Swiss roll, using the baking parchment to help turn it over. Trim off the ends of the roll, place on a serving plate, dust with icing sugar and decorate with mint leaves.

6 To serve, cut the meringue roll into slices and serve with the daiquiri sauce. The roll will keep for up to 24 hours in the fridge.

DOMINIC'S POACHED PEARS WITH GORGONZOLA CHEESECAKE

This recipe is from my friend Dominic who is a TV cameraman and an avid cook. He serves this dish at dinner parties **AS AN ALTERNATIVE TO A CHEESE COURSE**, and I must say it's really good. The sweetness of the pears and sauce balances out the saltiness of the cheese perfectly.

SERVES 8

For the cheesecake

65g unsalted butter, plus
   extra for greasing
180g digestive biscuits
250g mascarpone cheese
150g Gorgonzola dolce cheese
200ml double cream
8 peeled or candied walnut halves

For the pears

4 Conference pears, peeled
400ml red wine
350ml port
1 cinnamon stick
4 cloves
1 star anise
100ml clear blossom honey

1 Butter a 23cm loose-bottomed tin.

2 Place the pears in a deep saucepan, add the wine, port, spices and honey and cover with a piece of greaseproof paper. Bring to the boil, lower the heat and simmer until the pears are tender – about 12 minutes. Remove the pears using a slotted spoon and set aside to cool.

3 Return the pan to the heat, boil rapidly until the poaching liquid is reduced by two-thirds or until it has a sticky sauce consistency. Set aside to cool.

4 Blitz the biscuits in a food processor to form fine crumbs. Melt the butter in a large saucepan and stir in the crumbs. Spoon the mixture into the prepared tin and press evenly over the base. Chill in the fridge for at least 30 minutes.

5 Put the mascarpone and Gorgonzola in a mixing bowl and beat together until combined. In a separate bowl whip the double cream until it just holds its shape and then fold into the cheese mixture.

6 Cover the biscuit base with the cheese mixture and smooth with a palette knife, then chill in the fridge for at least 1 hour.

7 To assemble, remove the cheesecake from the tin, decorate with the walnut halves and cut into 8 slices. Take a pear, halve and core, then slice each half into a fan and place on a plate with a slice of cheesecake. Finish with a spoon of the wine and port reduction.

SWEET RICE ARANCINI WITH COCONUT AND MANGO

Arancini is a wonderful savoury treat and here's a delicious dessert version. These

FRAGRANT SWEET RICE BALLS are really moreish and great as a dessert or

even as a sweet snack. I love the Caribbean flavours.

SERVES 4

1 lemongrass stalk
200ml coconut milk
½ vanilla pod, split
200ml double cream
50ml Malibu (coconut rum)
75g pudding rice
2 free-range egg yolks
75g caster sugar
1 ripe mango, peeled and cut into
    1cm cubes
2 tablespoons plain flour, for dusting
1 free-range egg, beaten
75g desiccated coconut
vegetable oil, for deep frying
dark chocolate sauce, to serve

1 Bruise the lemongrass using a rolling pin. Put it in a medium heavy-based saucepan with the coconut milk, split vanilla pod, cream and Malibu. Bring slowly to the boil before adding the rice. Return to the boil then simmer gently, stirring occasionally, until nearly all of the liquid has been absorbed.

2 Beat the egg yolks and sugar together in a large bowl. Gradually add the rice mixture to the egg and sugar mixture. Return everything to the pan and continue to gently heat until the rice has thickened.

3 Remove the pan from the heat and tip the rice into a clean, large mixing bowl. Set aside to cool. Once at room temperature chill in the fridge for at least 1 hour.

4 Remove the rice from the fridge and with wet hands take 1 tablespoon of the mixture, moulding it into a ball in your hand. Push your finger into the middle of the ball, then pop in a cube of the mango. Seal the hole with more rice, squeezing and rolling the arancini into a ball, about the size of a golf ball. Place on a baking tray lined with baking parchment. Repeat to make 8 balls. Place the arancini in the fridge to chill for at least 30 minutes.

5 Remove the arancini from the fridge and dust all over with the flour. Dip them in the beaten egg, then roll in the desiccated coconut, ensuring they are thoroughly coated. Chill for at least a further 30 minutes.

6 Heat the oil in a medium heavy-based saucepan to 160°C. Fry the arancini in batches of 4 until they are golden – about 4–5 minutes. Remove using a slotted spoon and place on a plate lined with kitchen paper, to drain. Serve with dark chocolate sauce or just enjoy as a sweet snack.

OREO COOKIE AND BLUEBERRY CHEESECAKE

A really simple-to-prepare **BAKED CHEESECAKE WITH A CRUSHED OREO**

COOKIE BASE and creamy blueberry filling. This was inspired by my time in the US

– it's vintage Americana in a cheesecake!

SERVES 8

70g butter, plus extra for greasing
200g Oreo cookies, roughly crushed
500g low-fat cream cheese
397g can condensed milk
seeds from 1 vanilla pod
3 free-range eggs
150g blueberries

1 Preheat the oven to 160°C/325°F/gas mark 3. Line and grease a 23cm loose-bottomed cake tin with baking parchment.

2 Melt the butter in a medium saucepan, stir in the crushed cookies until they are coated and start to stick together. Spoon the mix into the tin and press evenly over the base. Chill in the fridge for at least 30 minutes.

3 Beat the cream cheese in a mixing bowl until smooth, then add the condensed milk, seeds scraped from the vanilla pod and eggs. Beat well until evenly combined.

4 Pour the filling over the biscuit base and sprinkle the blueberries over the top. Bake for 1 hour or until set. Remove and set aside to cool then chill in the fridge and serve.

CHOCOLATE AND ORANGE TART

A ready-made sweet pastry case spread with orange marmalade and **TOPPED WITH A**

RICH DARK CHOCOLATE FILLING. The marmalade gives this tart its twist, adding a

pleasantly sour hint which works brilliantly with the chocolate. It's very quick to prepare, too.

SERVES 4–6

320g dark chocolate
(55–60% cocoa solids)
1 x 25cm ready-made sweet shortcrust
pastry case
200g unsalted butter
60g caster sugar
2 free-range eggs
150g thick cut marmalade
mascarpone cheese or clotted cream,
to serve

1 Preheat the oven to 160°C/320°F/gas mark 3.

2 Melt 20g of the chocolate in a small heatproof bowl over a saucepan of barely simmering water. Brush the chocolate over the pastry case and set aside in the fridge for the chocolate to set.

3 Melt the butter and rest of the chocolate in a large heatproof bowl over a saucepan of barely simmering water. Stir until melted and combined.

4 In another bowl whisk the sugar and eggs together. Stir the chocolate mixture into the egg mixture.

5 Spread the marmalade evenly over the base of the pastry case. Pour the chocolate filling evenly into the case.

6 Bake for 15 minutes. Remove from the oven and leave in the tin to cool on a wire rack. Serve at room temperature with mascarpone or clotted cream.

EASY CHOCOLATE COOKIE NUT SALAMI

The **PERFECT TREAT** at the end of a meal to serve with coffee. Experiment with

different biscuits for endless varieties of flavours! This is super easy to prepare and

requires no cooking. Just pop in the freezer and take a slice whenever you fancy!

MAKES 25 SLICES

180ml whipping cream

60g unsalted butter

50ml espresso (or 1 level teaspoon instant coffee mixed with 50ml boiling water)

1 teaspoon vanilla extract

155g dark chocolate chips

250g biscuits (digestives, oat cookies or rich tea)

100g mixed hazelnuts, walnuts and pistachios

pinch of salt

sifted icing sugar, for dusting

1 Put the cream, butter, coffee and vanilla extract in a small saucepan and bring to a simmer.

2 Put the chocolate chips into a large mixing bowl and pour over the hot cream mixture. Cover the bowl with clingfilm and leave to stand for 5 minutes.

3 Place the biscuits and nuts into a plastic food bag and smash into large chunks using a rolling pin.

4 Stir the cream and chocolate mixture until rich and glossy, tip in the biscuit and nut pieces, add the salt and stir well.

5 Pour the mixture onto a large rectangle of greaseproof paper, shape into a sausage and twist up both ends of the paper. Roll up the parcel in clingfilm to help the sausage hold its shape. Put in the freezer for 2 hours, or until solid.

6 When you are ready to serve, remove the clingfilm and peel away the paper. Place on a baking tray, dust and roll all over with icing sugar. Slice the chocolate salami into bite-sized pieces and serve with coffee after a meal.

7 Store the chocolate salami in the freezer and slice as required.

BLACK FOREST BROWNIES

Black Forest gâteau crossed with chocolate brownies. The black cherries soak up the

cherry liqueur to produce **A BIG HIT OF FRUITY FLAVOUR IN EACH BITE**.

Serve as a pudding with a scoop of ice cream or for afternoon tea with lashings of cream.

SERVES 8

160g unsalted butter, plus extra
   for greasing
150g fresh black cherries, pitted
   and halved
3 tablespoons cherry liqueur
150g dark chocolate (55–60%
   cocoa solids)
140g milk chocolate
3 free-range eggs
165g caster sugar
85g soft plain flour, sifted

1 Preheat the oven to 180°C/350°F/gas mark 4. Grease and line a
25 x 20cm baking tin with baking parchment.

2 Place the cherries in a small bowl and cover with the cherry
liqueur. Set aside to macerate for at least 10 minutes.

3 Melt the chocolate and butter in a large heatproof bowl over
a saucepan of barely simmering water. Once melted, stir the
chocolate and butter until smooth.

4 Put the eggs and sugar in a medium bowl and whisk using an
electric whisk until pale and doubled in size.

5 Gently fold the whisked egg mixture into the melted chocolate.
When fully incorporated, fold in the sifted flour. Fold the cherries
and liqueur into the brownie mixture. Pour the mixture into the tin
and smooth over the top to even the surface.

6 Bake for 20 minutes, then remove and leave in the tin to cool on
a wire rack. Cut into 8 pieces.

FIG, SHERRY AND CHOCOLATE PAVLOVA

Gooey pavlova topped with **SHERRY-SOAKED FIGS AND VANILLA CREAM**

and served with dark chocolate sauce. This grown-up dish is an impressive dessert

for dinner parties – it looks stunning but is actually easy to create.

SERVES 4

5 free-range egg whites
pinch of salt
250g caster sugar, plus 1 teaspoon
2 teaspoons cornflour
1 teaspoon white wine vinegar
pinch of cream of tartar
8 fresh figs
1 vanilla pod
120ml dry sherry
1 tablespoon clear blossom honey
320ml double cream
25g dark chocolate (72% cocoa solids),
  roughly chopped

1 Preheat the oven to 150°C/300°F/gas mark 2. Draw a 25cm circle on a piece of baking parchment and place it on a baking sheet.

2 Put the egg whites in a large clean bowl with the salt and 125g of the sugar and whisk until doubled in size. Now gradually add the remaining sugar, whisking until the mixture is stiff and glossy. Fold in the cornflour, white wine vinegar and cream of tartar.

3 Spoon the mixture evenly into the circle of baking parchment. Bake the pavlova for 1 hour 15 minutes or until it has a crisp coating and comes away from the baking parchment without sticking. Peel the baking parchment off and place the pavlova on a baking sheet on a wire rack and set aside to cool.

4 Trim the figs stalks and cut a cross in the top of each fig. Gently squeeze open each fig and place into a bowl. Split the vanilla pod, scrape out the seeds and set aside.

5 Heat the sherry, honey and scraped-out vanilla pod in a saucepan. Bring to boiling point then pour over the figs. Cover the bowl with clingfilm and set aside for the figs to steam and soak up the liquid.

6 Put 70ml of the cream in a small non-stick saucepan over a medium heat, add the dark chocolate, stir until fully melted but don't let it boil.

7 Whisk the remaining cream with 1 teaspoon of caster sugar and the vanilla seeds until stiff peaks form.

8 To serve, spread the vanilla cream over the pavlova. Drain the figs and arrange on top of the cream. Finish with a drizzle of chocolate sauce or serve separately.

CHOCOLATE AND HAZELNUT PUDDINGS

An indulgent variation on the **CLASSIC BREAD PUDDING** – individual chocolate

puds with hazelnut praline. It's like your favourite chocolate and hazelnut spread

in a dessert!

SERVES 4

For the praline
100g caster sugar
100g chopped hazelnuts

For the pudding
butter, for greasing
6 slices white bread, crusts removed
150g dark chocolate (55–60% cocoa
    solids), broken into pieces
600ml whole milk
seeds from 1 vanilla pod
4 free-range eggs
25g caster sugar
1 teaspoon cocoa powder

1 Put the sugar and nuts in a small heavy-based saucepan over a medium heat until the sugar melts and starts to caramelise, stirring to coat the nuts. Once the caramel browns, pour the mixture onto a non-stick baking sheet, spread out and leave to cool. Once cooled and set, smash the praline into roughly 0.5cm pieces with a toffee hammer or rolling pin or pulse in a blender.

2 Preheat the oven to 180°C/350°F/gas mark 4. Lightly butter 4 100ml ramekins or 4 teacups.

3 Tear or cut the bread into roughly 2cm pieces. Put in a bowl with the praline and half the chocolate, stir well to combine and divide between the 4 dishes.

4 Put the milk in a small saucepan with the seeds scraped from the vanilla pod and the remaining chocolate. Gently heat until the chocolate has melted and the mixture is just warm. Whisk together the eggs, sugar and cocoa powder in a medium jug, pour in the warm chocolate milk and whisk well.

5 Pour the chocolate milk into the dishes and lightly press down the bread so that it absorbs the liquid. Leave for 2 minutes.

6 Place the dishes in a roasting tin and pour hot water into the tin to come two-thirds of the way up the dishes. Bake for 30 minutes. To test if the puddings are cooked, cut one with a small knife and check there is no liquid in the bottom of the ramekin. If any liquid remains, bake for a further 10 minutes. Once cooked, remove the dishes from the tin and leave to stand for 10 minutes. Serve in the dishes or turned out, if you prefer.

CHOKE AND WHITE CHOCOLATE TART

I came up with this sweet and savoury mix of white chocolate and **JERUSALEM ARTICHOKE**

when I had some leftover artichoke purée one day. Somehow the flavours work brilliantly together –

the sweetness of the chocolate balancing the earthiness of the artichoke. Who would have thought?

SERVES 6

200g Jerusalem artichokes
500ml whole milk
100g white chocolate, roughly chopped
6 free-range egg yolks
50g caster sugar
1 x 20cm ready-made sweet shortcrust
   pastry case

1 Preheat the oven to 150°C/300°F/gas mark 2.

2 Peel and thinly slice the artichokes, put in a small saucepan with the milk and bring to the boil. Gently simmer for 10 minutes or until the artichokes are soft. Transfer to a food processor, blend together and pass through a fine sieve. Stir in the white chocolate and set aside to cool slightly.

3 Whisk together the egg yolks and sugar in a large bowl until smooth and pale. Pour in the artichoke and chocolate mixture and whisk. Pour the custard into the pastry case and cook for 20–25 minutes until just set.

4 Remove and set aside to cool for 2 hours to room temperature before slicing to serve.

CHOKE AND WHITE CHOCOLATE TART (Recipe on page 167)

CHRISTMAS TART

A festive dessert of **SWEET MINCEMEAT AND FRANGIPANE** baked in a tart

shell and finished with glacé icing. Try this twist on Bakewell tart for something totally

different at Christmas, or just if you have some leftover mincemeat in the cupboard.

SERVES 6

125g unsalted butter, at room
   temperature
125g caster sugar
125g ground almonds
3 free-range eggs
2 tablespoons rum
200g mincemeat
1 x 25cm ready-made sweet shortcrust
   pastry case
3 tablespoons icing sugar
custard, to serve

1 Preheat the oven to 180°C/350°F/gas mark 4.

2 Cream together the butter and sugar in a mixing bowl. Add the ground almonds, eggs and rum and beat until well combined.

3 Spread the mincemeat over the base of the pastry case. Place the almond mixture in a piping bag with the tip cut to 1.5cm or fitted with a 1.5cm nozzle and pipe it over the mincemeat.

4 Bake for 30 minutes until golden, then cool on a wire rack.

5 Mix the icing sugar with 1 teaspoon water and stir well. Drizzle the icing over the tart and leave to set for 10 minutes.

6 Serve the tart at room temperature with warm custard.

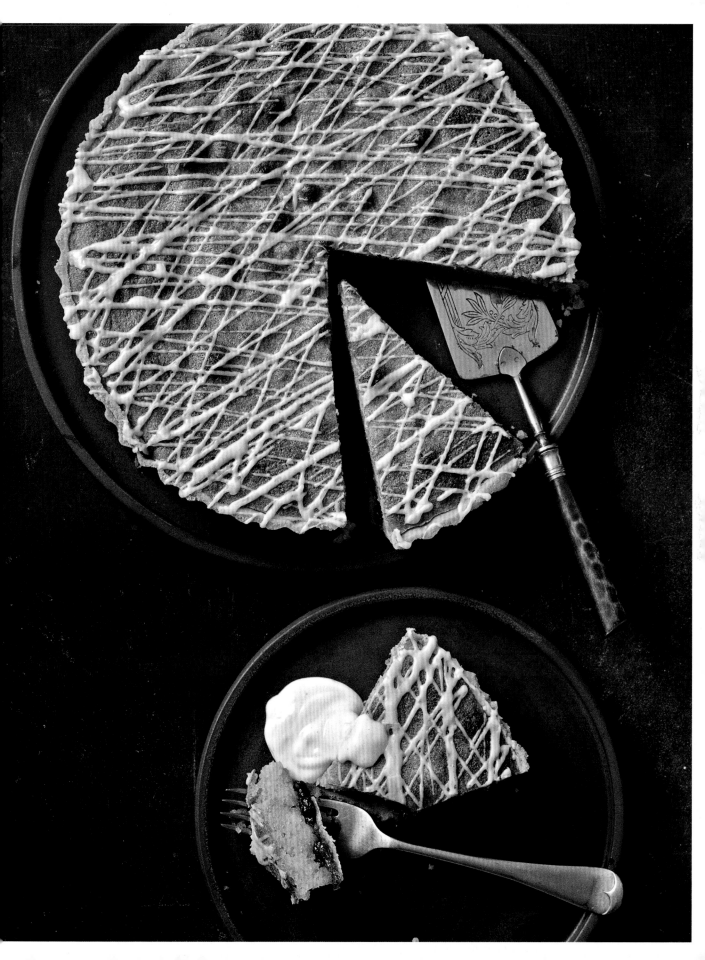

INDEX